SARA L. WESTON

Authenticity Unveiled: Creating our Authentic Selves

Contents

Foreword

All of the concepts, ideas and skills in this book are derived from the clinical psychology literature, research and theory, as well as best practice in clinical psychology and are used by therapists worldwide.

As an author I strive to give the reader a combination of embracing brevity with substance. My books are therefore different to many other self help manuals and authors. Often times readers start out with good intentions of completing a book, but competing interests get in the way. So often getting through entire self help workbooks is required to gain insight and make improvements in one's life . For some readers, not completing a book can leave them feeling despondent and unmotivated. It is my hope that the reader absorbs a lot, in a short space of time, and therefore, quickly gains insight and perspective, which motivates the reader to embrace change towards creating their authentic selves. When they can see positive change is possible, they continue their journey towards self improvement. This book can be read as a stand alone, or in combination as a companion with other books in the same genre. This gives the reader an opportunity for a deeper level of understanding and change.

Preface

This book is for anyone who has ever felt they are living their life for the validation and respect of someone else. If they've ever felt the pain of a fractured relationship, the sting of rejection, or the yearning for deeper, more meaningful connections with someone who gets you!. It's for those who want to break free from toxic patterns and embrace a future filled with genuine love, acceptance, and understanding. Whether you're struggling in romantic partnerships, familial relationships, or friendships, "Authenticity Unveiled" offers a road-map to building authentic, lasting bonds that bring joy, fulfillment, and harmony into your life.

As the author, I invite you to approach this journey with an open mind and heart and a willingness to explore the depths of your own authenticity, embracing the good parts of yourself and the not so good. Your relationship with yourself is the cornerstone upon which all other relationships are built. The insights you gain and the transformations you undergo will not only improve your relationships with yourself, but also your connections with others and lead to a more fulfilling and harmonious life.

Sara

I

Part One

Book Overview
In "Authenticity Unveiled" the author explores the concept of self-acceptance as the foundation for building healthy and fulfilling relationships. The book offers practical strategies and insights to help readers navigate the complexities of relationships and cultivate authenticity. By understanding and embracing their own worth, readers will learn how to set boundaries, communicate effectively, and create healthy relationships.

1

Chapter 1

Understanding Relationship Dynamics

1.1 Recognizing Patterns in Relationships

In order to build real and lasting relationships, it is crucial to first recognize the patterns that exist within our interactions with others. Our closest relationships, whether they be romantic, familial, or platonic, can often become a source of crisis rather than solace. We may find ourselves stuck in repetitive cycles, where we desire change but struggle to break free from the familiar patterns that keep us trapped.

These patterns can manifest in various ways. For example, in romantic relationships, we may repeatedly find ourselves attracted to partners who are emotionally unavailable or who exhibit unhealthy behaviors. In familial relationships, we may constantly fall into the same patterns of conflict or feel trapped in roles that limit our growth. Even in friendships or workplace relationships, we may notice recurring themes of power imbalances or communication breakdowns.

Recognizing these patterns is the first step towards understanding the dynamics at play within our relationships. It requires a willingness to reflect on our own behaviors and choices, as well as an openness to examining the role we play in perpetuating these patterns. By gaining awareness of these patterns, we can begin to break free from them and create healthier, more fulfilling connections.

One way to recognize patterns in relationships is to reflect on our past experiences. By examining our history, we can identify common themes or behaviors that have emerged in our interactions with others. This may involve looking at our childhood experiences and the dynamics within our family of origin, as these early relationships often shape our patterns of relating later in life.

Another helpful tool is to pay attention to our emotional reactions and responses within relationships. Do we find ourselves feeling consistently anxious, frustrated, or unfulfilled? Are there certain triggers or situations that consistently lead to conflict or disconnection? By tuning into our emotions, we can gain valuable insights into the patterns that are at play.

It is also important to consider the role of communication in relationship patterns. Communication is the foundation of any healthy connection, and the way we communicate can either reinforce or disrupt patterns. Are we effectively expressing our needs and desires? Are we actively listening and empathizing with others? Are we engaging in open and honest dialogue, or are we avoiding difficult conversations? By examining our communication styles, we can uncover patterns that may be hindering our relationships.

Furthermore, power dynamics often play a significant role in relationship patterns. Power imbalances can lead to feelings of resentment, inequality, and a lack of autonomy. It is important to examine whether we are giving away our power or allowing others to dominate us, as this can perpetuate unhealthy patterns. By recognizing and addressing power imbalances, we can create more equitable and balanced relationships.

Identifying unhealthy relationship habits is another crucial aspect of recognizing patterns. These habits can include codependency, enabling destructive behaviors, or engaging in toxic communication patterns. By acknowledging these habits, we can begin to break free from them and develop healthier ways of relating.

In conclusion, recognizing patterns in relationships is an essential step towards building real and lasting connections. By reflecting on our past experiences, examining our emotional reactions, considering our communication styles, addressing power dynamics, and identifying unhealthy habits, we can gain a deeper understanding of the dynamics at play within our relationships. This awareness empowers us to break free from destructive patterns and cultivate healthier, more fulfilling connections with others.

1.2 Exploring the Role of Communication

Communication is a fundamental aspect of human interaction and plays a crucial role in the dynamics of relationships. It serves as the foundation for understanding, connection, and the resolution of conflicts. In order to build real and lasting relationships, it is essential to explore and understand the role that communication plays in shaping our interactions with others.

The Power of Effective Communication

Effective communication is the key to fostering healthy and fulfilling relationships. It involves not only expressing oneself clearly but also actively listening and understanding others. When communication is open, honest, and respectful, it creates an environment where individuals feel heard, valued, and understood.

One of the primary benefits of effective communication is the ability to express emotions, needs, and desires in a constructive manner. By openly sharing our thoughts and feelings, we allow others to gain insight into our inner world, fostering empathy and connection. This level of vulnerability and authenticity strengthens the bond between individuals and promotes a deeper understanding of each other's perspectives.

Breaking Down Barriers

In order to explore the role of communication in relationships, it is important to identify and address the barriers that hinder effective communication. These barriers can manifest in various forms, such as misunderstandings, misinterpretations, and emotional blocks.

One common barrier to effective communication is a lack of active listening. Often, individuals are more focused on formulating their response rather than truly hearing what the other person is saying. This can lead to miscommunication and a failure to fully understand each other's viewpoints. Active listening involves giving one's full attention, maintaining eye contact, and providing verbal and non-verbal cues to show understanding and engagement.

Another barrier is the presence of emotional blocks. Past experiences, insecurities, and fears can create emotional barriers that prevent individuals from expressing themselves openly and honestly. These emotional blocks can lead to defensive or aggressive communication styles, hindering the development of healthy relationships. It is important to recognize and address these emotional barriers through self-reflection, therapy, or other forms of personal growth.

The Role of Non-Verbal Communication

Communication extends beyond words alone. Non-verbal cues, such as body language, facial expressions, and tone of voice, play a significant role in conveying messages and emotions. In fact, research suggests that non-verbal communication accounts for a substantial portion of our overall communication.

Being aware of and attuned to non-verbal cues can enhance the effectiveness of communication. For example, maintaining eye contact and open body language can signal attentiveness and interest. Conversely, crossed arms or a tense posture may indicate defensiveness or discomfort. Understanding and interpreting these non-verbal cues can help individuals navigate conversations and respond appropriately.

Conflict Resolution through Communication

Conflict is an inevitable part of any relationship. However, how conflicts are addressed and resolved can significantly impact the health and longevity of the relationship. Effective communication plays a vital role in resolving conflicts in a constructive and respectful manner.

When conflicts arise, it is important to approach them with a willingness to listen and understand the other person's perspective. Active listening, empathy, and open-mindedness can help de-escalate tensions and foster a collaborative approach to finding solutions. It is crucial to avoid blame, criticism, and defensiveness, as these can further exacerbate conflicts and hinder effective communication.

The Importance of Assertive Communication

Assertive communication is a valuable skill that promotes healthy relationships. It involves expressing one's thoughts, feelings, and needs in a clear and respectful manner while also considering the rights and perspectives of others. Assertive communication allows individuals to assert their boundaries, express their desires, and address conflicts without resorting to aggression or passivity.

By practicing assertive communication, individuals can establish open and honest lines of communication, fostering trust and mutual respect. It enables individuals to advocate for themselves while also valuing the opinions and needs of others. This balanced approach to communication promotes healthy relationship dynamics and paves the way for effective problem-solving and compromise.

Cultivating Effective Communication Skills

Developing effective communication skills is an ongoing process that requires self-awareness, practice, and a willingness to learn and grow. Here are some strategies to cultivate effective communication in relationships:

1. Active Listening: Practice active listening by giving your full attention, maintaining eye contact, and providing verbal and non-verbal cues to show understanding and engagement.

2. Emotional Awareness: Reflect on your emotional blocks and insecurities that may hinder open and honest communication. Seek therapy or engage in self-reflection to address these barriers.

3. Non-Verbal Cues: Pay attention to non-verbal cues, such as body language and tone of voice, to better understand the emotions and messages being conveyed.

4. Conflict Resolution: Approach conflicts with a willingness to listen and understand the other person's perspective. Practice empathy, open-mindedness, and avoid blame or defensiveness.

5. Assertive Communication: Develop assertive communication skills to express your thoughts, feelings, and needs in a clear and respectful manner while considering the rights and perspectives of others.

By actively exploring and improving our communication skills, we can create a solid foundation for building real and lasting relationships. Effective communication fosters understanding, connection, and mutual growth, allowing individuals to navigate the complexities of relationships with greater ease and fulfillment.

1.3 Understanding Power Dynamics

In order to build real and lasting relationships, it is crucial to understand the dynamics of power within those relationships. Power dynamics refer to the ways in which power is distributed, exercised, and negotiated between individuals. These dynamics can greatly influence the health and stability of a relationship, as well as the overall satisfaction and well-being of those involved.

Power imbalances can manifest in various ways within relationships. It is important to recognize that power does not necessarily equate to control or dominance. Power can be both positive and negative, and it can be shared or unevenly distributed between individuals. Understanding power dynamics involves acknowledging the different sources and expressions of power within a relationship.

One common source of power within relationships is personal power. Personal power refers to an individual's ability to assert their needs, desires, and boundaries. It involves having a sense of self-worth, confidence, and autonomy. When both individuals in a relationship have a healthy sense of personal power, it creates a balanced and mutually respectful dynamic.

However, power imbalances can occur when one person in the relationship consistently dominates or controls the other. This can lead to feelings of powerlessness, resentment, and a lack of agency for the person on the receiving end. It is important to be aware of these imbalances and address them in order to foster a healthy and equitable relationship.

Another aspect of power dynamics is social power, which refers to the influence and authority that individuals hold within their social contexts. This can include factors such as gender, race, socioeconomic status, and other societal hierarchies. Social power imbalances can impact relationships by perpetuating inequalities and creating barriers to effective communication and understanding.

For example, in a romantic relationship, gender roles and societal expectations can influence power dynamics. Traditional gender norms may assign more power and decision-making authority to one gender over the other. This can lead to unequal distribution of power and contribute to feelings of inequality and dissatisfaction within the relationship.

Power dynamics can also be influenced by past experiences and traumas. Individuals who have experienced abuse or trauma may struggle with asserting their personal power and setting boundaries in relationships. This can create a power imbalance where one person feels entitled to control or manipulate the other. Understanding and addressing these underlying issues is crucial for creating a safe and healthy relationship.

It is important to note that power dynamics are not inherently negative or destructive. In fact, power imbalances can be addressed and transformed into a more equitable and mutually beneficial dynamic. This requires open and honest communication, empathy, and a willingness to challenge and change unhealthy patterns.

To understand power dynamics within a relationship, it is essential to engage in self-reflection and self-awareness. This involves examining one's own beliefs, values, and behaviors that may contribute to power imbalances. It also requires actively listening to and validating the experiences and perspectives of the other person in the relationship.

Effective communication is key in navigating power dynamics. It is important to create a safe and non-judgmental space where both individuals can express their needs, concerns, and boundaries. Active listening, empathy, and validation are essential in fostering understanding and addressing power imbalances.

Building real and lasting relationships requires a commitment to equality, respect, and mutual growth. By understanding and addressing power dynamics, individuals can create healthier and more fulfilling relationships. It is an ongoing process that requires self-reflection, open communication, and a willingness to challenge and change unhealthy patterns.

1.4 Identifying Unhealthy Relationship Habits

In order to build real and lasting relationships, it is crucial to identify and address unhealthy relationship habits. These habits can hinder personal growth, create emotional distress, and prevent the development of healthy connections with others. Unfortunately, many individuals find themselves trapped in patterns of behavior that perpetuate these unhealthy habits, leading to dissatisfaction and conflict in their relationships.

Unhealthy relationship habits can manifest in various ways, and it is important to recognize them in order to break free from their negative impact. Here are some common unhealthy relationship habits to be aware of:

1. Lack of Communication

One of the most detrimental habits in any relationship is a lack of communication. When individuals fail to express their thoughts, feelings, and needs openly and honestly, it can lead to misunderstandings, resentment, and a breakdown in trust. Effective communication is the foundation of any healthy relationship, and without it, conflicts can escalate and intimacy can suffer.

2. Poor Conflict Resolution Skills

Conflict is a natural part of any relationship, but how it is handled can make all the difference. Unhealthy relationship habits often involve poor conflict resolution skills, such as avoiding conflict altogether, becoming defensive, or resorting to aggression. These behaviors can create a toxic environment and prevent the resolution of issues, leading to ongoing tension and resentment.

3. Lack of Boundaries

Boundaries are essential for maintaining healthy relationships. When individuals fail to establish and enforce their personal boundaries, it can result in feelings of being taken advantage of, resentment, and a loss of self-identity. Unhealthy relationship habits often involve a lack of respect for boundaries, whether it be emotional, physical, or personal space boundaries.

4. Codependency

Codependency is a dysfunctional pattern of behavior where individuals excessively rely on each other for emotional support and validation. This unhealthy relationship habit can lead to a loss of personal autonomy, a lack of self-esteem, and an inability to establish healthy boundaries. Codependent relationships often involve enabling behaviors, a fear of abandonment, and an imbalance of power dynamics.

5. Emotional Manipulation

Emotional manipulation is a toxic habit that can erode trust and emotional well-being in a relationship. It involves using tactics such as guilt-tripping, gaslighting, or playing mind games to control or manipulate the other person's emotions and actions. This unhealthy habit can lead to feelings of confusion, self-doubt, and a loss of personal agency.

6. Lack of Empathy

Empathy is the ability to understand and share the feelings of another person. When individuals lack empathy in a relationship, it can result in a lack of emotional support, invalidation of feelings, and a failure to connect on a deeper level. This unhealthy habit can create a sense of emotional distance and hinder the development of intimacy and trust.

7. Disrespectful Behavior

Respect is a fundamental aspect of any healthy relationship. Unhealthy relationship habits often involve disrespectful behavior, such as name-calling, belittling, or dismissing the thoughts and feelings of the other person. This habit can lead to a breakdown in communication, a loss of trust, and a deterioration of the relationship over time.

8. Control and Power Struggles

Unhealthy relationship habits can also manifest in control and power struggles. When individuals seek to exert control over their partner or engage in power struggles, it can create a toxic and imbalanced dynamic. This habit can lead to feelings of resentment, a loss of personal autonomy, and a lack of mutual respect.

Identifying these unhealthy relationship habits is the first step towards building healthier connections with others. By recognizing these patterns, individuals can begin to take responsibility for their own behavior and work towards creating positive change in their relationships. It is important to remember that change takes time and effort, but with dedication and self-reflection, it is possible to break free from these unhealthy habits and cultivate real and lasting relationships based on love, respect, and mutual growth.

2

Chapter 2

The Importance of Self-Love

2.1 Defining Self-Love

Self-love is a concept that has gained significant attention in recent years, and for good reason. It is the foundation upon which healthy and fulfilling relationships are built. But what exactly does self-love mean?

At its core, self-love is about having a deep and unconditional regard for oneself. It involves accepting and embracing all aspects of who you are, including your strengths, weaknesses, and imperfections. Self-love is not about being self-centered or narcissistic; rather, it is about recognizing your own worth and treating yourself with kindness, compassion, and respect.

Self-love is a journey of self-discovery and self-acceptance. It requires a willingness to explore your inner world, confront your fears and insecurities, and make a conscious effort to prioritize your own well-being. It is about recognizing that you are deserving of love, happiness, and fulfillment, just as much as anyone else.

In a society that often emphasizes the importance of external validation and approval, practicing self-love can be challenging. We are bombarded with messages that tell us we need to look a certain way, achieve certain goals, or possess certain material possessions in order to be worthy of love and acceptance. However, true self-love is not dependent on external factors or the opinions of others. It is an internal state of being that comes from within.

Self-love is about setting healthy boundaries and saying no when necessary. It is about prioritizing your own needs and desires without feeling guilty or selfish. It is about recognizing that you are responsible for your own happiness and well-being, and that it is not the job of others to fulfill these needs for you.

Practicing self-love involves taking care of your physical, emotional, and mental health. It means nourishing your body with nutritious food, engaging in regular exercise, and getting enough rest and relaxation. It also means taking time for self-reflection, engaging in activities that bring you joy and fulfillment, and surrounding yourself with positive and supportive people.

Self-love is not a destination; it is an ongoing process. It requires consistent effort and self-awareness. It means being gentle with yourself when you make mistakes or face challenges, and treating yourself with the same kindness and compassion you would offer to a loved one.

When you cultivate self-love, you become more resilient and better equipped to navigate the complexities of relationships. You are less likely to seek validation and approval from others, as you already have a strong sense of self-worth. This allows you to enter into relationships from a place of authenticity and confidence, rather than from a place of neediness or insecurity.

Self-love also enables you to set healthy boundaries in your relationships. You are able to communicate your needs and desires effectively, and you are less likely to tolerate behaviors that are disrespectful or harmful. By valuing and respecting yourself, you attract people who will do the same.

Furthermore, self-love allows you to be more present and engaged in your relationships. When you are secure in yourself and your worth, you are able to fully show up for others and offer them your love and support. You are able to give and receive love in a healthy and balanced way, without losing yourself in the process.

In summary, self-love is the foundation for building real and lasting relationships. It involves accepting and embracing yourself fully, setting healthy boundaries, and prioritizing your own well-being. By practicing self-love, you cultivate a deep sense of self-worth and authenticity, which allows you to engage in relationships from a place of love, respect, and fulfillment. Self love is about creating out authentic selves.

2.2 Exploring the Benefits of Self-Love

In our quest for fulfilling and lasting relationships, it is essential to recognize the profound impact that self-love can have on our interactions with others. Self-love is not a selfish or narcissistic concept; rather, it is the foundation upon which healthy relationships are built. When we cultivate a deep sense of self-love, we are better equipped to navigate the complexities of human connection and create meaningful bonds with others.

The Power of Self-Love

Self-love is the practice of nurturing and caring for oneself on a deep emotional and psychological level. It involves accepting and embracing all aspects of who we are, including our strengths, weaknesses, and imperfections. When we truly love ourselves, we develop a strong sense of self-worth and self-respect, which radiates into every area of our lives, including our relationships.

1. Increased Emotional Resilience

One of the significant benefits of self-love is increased emotional resilience. When we love ourselves, we are better equipped to handle the ups and downs of relationships without becoming overwhelmed or losing ourselves in the process. We develop a solid foundation of self-assurance and self-compassion, allowing us to bounce back from setbacks and conflicts with grace and resilience.

2. Authenticity and Vulnerability

Self-love empowers us to embrace our authentic selves and show up in relationships as our truest selves. When we love and accept ourselves, we no longer feel the need to wear masks or pretend to be someone we're not. This authenticity fosters deeper connections with others, as they can sense our genuine nature and feel safe to be vulnerable in return. By embracing vulnerability, we create an environment where trust and intimacy can flourish.

3. Healthy Boundaries

Self-love is closely intertwined with the establishment of healthy boundaries. When we love ourselves, we recognize our worth and value, and we are more likely to set and enforce boundaries that protect our emotional well-being. By clearly communicating our needs and limits, we create a space where mutual respect and understanding can thrive. Healthy boundaries foster healthier and more balanced relationships, as they prevent resentment and enable open and honest communication.

4. Improved Communication

Self-love plays a crucial role in enhancing our communication skills. When we love ourselves, we develop a deep sense of self-awareness and self-acceptance. This self-awareness allows us to recognize and express our emotions and needs effectively. Additionally, self-love enables us to listen attentively and empathetically to others, fostering a deeper understanding and connection. By cultivating self-love, we become better communicators, leading to more harmonious and fulfilling relationships.

5. Enhanced Emotional Well-being

Self-love is a powerful tool for enhancing our overall emotional well-being. When we prioritize self-love, we engage in self-care practices that nourish our mind, body, and soul. This self-care includes activities such as practicing mindfulness, engaging in hobbies we enjoy, setting aside time for relaxation, and surrounding ourselves with positive influences. By prioritizing our emotional well-being, we bring a sense of fulfillment and contentment into our relationships, allowing them to thrive.

6. Attracting Healthy Relationships

When we cultivate self-love, we naturally attract healthier and more fulfilling relationships into our lives. By valuing and respecting ourselves, we set a standard for the treatment we expect from others. We become less likely to tolerate toxic or unhealthy dynamics, and instead, we gravitate towards relationships that align with our values and support our growth. Self-love acts as a magnet, drawing in individuals who appreciate and cherish us for who we truly are.

7. Personal Growth and Development

Self-love is a catalyst for personal growth and development. When we love ourselves, we are motivated to explore our passions, pursue our dreams, and continuously evolve as individuals. This personal growth not only benefits us but also enriches our relationships. As we become more self-aware and self-assured, we bring a sense of purpose and fulfillment into our interactions with others, inspiring them to embark on their own journeys of growth.

In conclusion, self-love is a transformative force that has the power to revolutionize our relationships. By cultivating self-love, we unlock a myriad of benefits, including increased emotional resilience, authenticity, healthy boundaries, improved communication, enhanced emotional well-being, the attraction of healthy relationships, and personal growth. Embracing self-love is not only an act of self-care but also an act of love towards those we hold dear. When we love ourselves, we create a solid foundation upon which we can build real and lasting relationships.

2.3 Cultivating Self-Compassion

In our quest for building real and lasting relationships, it is essential to cultivate self-compassion. Self-compassion is the practice of treating ourselves with kindness, understanding, and acceptance, especially in times of difficulty or failure. It involves acknowledging our own suffering and extending the same compassion we would offer to a loved one towards ourselves.

The Importance of Self-Compassion

Self-compassion plays a crucial role in our ability to form healthy and fulfilling relationships. When we lack self-compassion, we tend to be overly critical of ourselves, which can lead to feelings of inadequacy and low self-esteem. This self-criticism can spill over into our relationships, causing us to project our insecurities onto others and creating unnecessary conflict and tension.

On the other hand, cultivating self-compassion allows us to approach relationships from a place of self-acceptance and understanding. It enables us to be more forgiving of our own mistakes and shortcomings, which in turn allows us to extend the same forgiveness and understanding to others. By practicing self-compassion, we create a foundation of empathy and kindness that can transform the dynamics of our relationships.

The Three Elements of Self-Compassion

Self-compassion consists of three interconnected elements: self-kindness, common humanity, and mindfulness.

1. Self-Kindness

Self-kindness involves treating ourselves with warmth, care, and under-standing, especially when we are facing challenges or setbacks. Instead of berating ourselves for our mistakes, we offer ourselves the same compassion and support we would offer to a dear friend. This gentle and nurturing approach allows us to heal and grow, fostering a sense of self-worth and resilience that positively impacts our relationships.

2. Common Humanity

The second element of self-compassion is recognizing our shared humanity. It is understanding that we are not alone in our struggles and that everyone experiences pain, failure, and imperfection. By acknowledging our common humanity, we cultivate a sense of connection and empathy towards others. This understanding helps us to approach our relationships with compassion and understanding, knowing that we are all on this journey together.

3. Mindfulness

Mindfulness is the third element of self-compassion. It involves being present in the moment and observing our thoughts and emotions without judgment. By practicing mindfulness, we can become aware of our self-critical thoughts and replace them with self-compassionate ones. Mind-fulness allows us to cultivate a non-reactive and non-judgmental stance towards ourselves, enabling us to respond to challenges and conflicts in our relationships with greater clarity and compassion.

Cultivating Self-Compassion

Cultivating self-compassion is a lifelong practice that requires patience, self-awareness, and self-care. Here are some strategies to help you cultivate self-compassion and enhance your relationships:

1. Practice Self-Care

Self-care is an essential aspect of self-compassion. Take time to nurture yourself physically, emotionally, and mentally. Engage in activities that bring you joy and relaxation. Prioritize your well-being and make self-care a non-negotiable part of your routine. By taking care of yourself, you are better equipped to show up fully in your relationships.

2. Challenge Self-Critical Thoughts

Become aware of your self-critical thoughts and challenge them with self-compassionate ones. When you notice yourself being overly critical or judgmental, pause and ask yourself how you would respond to a loved one in the same situation. Treat yourself with the same kindness and understanding you would offer to them. Remember that making mistakes and facing challenges is a natural part of being human.

3. Practice Mindfulness

Incorporate mindfulness into your daily life. Set aside time each day to engage in mindfulness meditation or simply practice being present in the moment. Notice your thoughts and emotions without judgment, allowing them to come and go. By cultivating mindfulness, you can develop a greater sense of self-awareness and respond to situations in your relationships with greater compassion and understanding.

4. Seek Support

Reach out to trusted friends, family members, or a therapist for support and guidance. Sharing your struggles and challenges with others can provide a fresh perspective and help you cultivate self-compassion. Surround yourself with people who uplift and support you, and who encourage your journey towards self-compassion and healthier relationships.

5. Practice Gratitude

Cultivate a gratitude practice to shift your focus towards the positive aspects of your life. Take time each day to reflect on the things you are grateful for, including your own strengths and qualities. By cultivating gratitude, you can foster a sense of self-appreciation and develop a more compassionate outlook towards yourself and others.

Embracing Self-Compassion for Lasting Relationships

Cultivating self-compassion is a transformative journey that can positively impact all areas of our lives, including our relationships. By treating ourselves with kindness, acknowledging our shared humanity, and practicing mindfulness, we create a solid foundation for building real and lasting connections with others. Embracing self-compassion allows us to approach relationships with empathy, understanding, and acceptance, fostering a deeper sense of love and connection.

2.4 Building Self-Esteem and Confidence

Building self-esteem and confidence is a crucial aspect of developing healthy and fulfilling relationships. When we have a strong sense of self-worth and belief in our abilities, we are better equipped to navigate the complexities of relationships and establish meaningful connections with others. In this section, we will explore various strategies and practices that can help you build and enhance your self-esteem and confidence.

Understanding Self-Esteem

Self-esteem refers to how we perceive and value ourselves. It is the foundation upon which our confidence is built. When we have healthy self-esteem, we have a positive self-image and believe in our inherent worthiness. On the other hand, low self-esteem can lead to self-doubt, negative self-talk, and a lack of confidence in our abilities.

Recognizing the Importance of Self-Acceptance

One of the first steps in building self-esteem and confidence is practicing self-acceptance. This involves embracing all aspects of ourselves, including our strengths, weaknesses, and imperfections. It means acknowledging that we are human and that it is okay to make mistakes and have flaws. By accepting ourselves as we are, we can cultivate a sense of self-worth that is not dependent on external validation.

Celebrating Your Achievements

Taking the time to acknowledge and celebrate your achievements is another powerful way to boost self-esteem and confidence. Whether big or small, every accomplishment deserves recognition. By celebrating your successes, you reinforce the belief in your abilities and build a positive self-image. This can be as simple as giving yourself a pat on the back or treating yourself to something special.

Challenging Negative Self-Talk

Negative self-talk can be a significant barrier to building self-esteem and confidence. It is essential to become aware of the negative thoughts and beliefs we hold about ourselves and challenge them. Whenever you catch yourself engaging in self-critical or self-deprecating thoughts, replace them with positive affirmations and reminders of your strengths and accomplishments. Over time, this practice can help rewire your thinking patterns and cultivate a more positive self-image.

Setting Realistic Goals

Setting realistic goals is an effective way to build self-esteem and confidence. When we set achievable goals and work towards them, we experience a sense of accomplishment and progress. Start by breaking down larger goals into smaller, manageable steps. Celebrate each milestone along the way, and use these achievements as evidence of your capabilities. As you achieve your goals, your self-esteem and confidence will naturally grow.

Surrounding Yourself with Positive Influences

The people we surround ourselves with can have a significant impact on our self-esteem and confidence. Seek out relationships and friendships with individuals who uplift and support you. Surrounding yourself with positive influences can help counteract negative self-perceptions and reinforce your sense of self-worth. Additionally, engaging in activities and hobbies that bring you joy and fulfillment can also contribute to building self-esteem and confidence.

Practicing Self-Care

Self-care is an essential component of building self-esteem and confidence. Taking care of your physical, emotional, and mental well-being sends a powerful message to yourself that you are deserving of love and attention. Engage in activities that nourish your mind, body, and soul, such as exercise, meditation, spending time in nature, or pursuing hobbies you enjoy. Prioritizing self-care allows you to recharge and replenish your energy, which in turn boosts your self-esteem and confidence.

Embracing Failure as a Learning Opportunity

Failure is an inevitable part of life, and how we perceive and respond to it can greatly impact our self-esteem and confidence. Instead of viewing failure as a reflection of your worth or abilities, see it as an opportunity for growth and learning. Embrace failure as a natural part of the journey towards success and use it as motivation to keep pushing forward. By reframing failure in this way, you can maintain a positive outlook and build resilience in the face of challenges.

Seeking Support

Building self-esteem and confidence is not always an easy task, and it can be helpful to seek support from trusted friends, family members, or professionals. Consider reaching out to a therapist or counselor who can provide guidance and tools to help you navigate the process. Surrounding yourself with a supportive network can provide encouragement, validation, and perspective as you work towards building self-esteem and confidence.

Remember, building self-esteem and confidence is a lifelong journey. It requires consistent effort, self-reflection, and self-compassion. By implementing these strategies and practices into your daily life, you can cultivate a strong sense of self-worth and confidence that will positively impact your relationships and overall well-being.

3

Chapter 3

Healing Past Wounds

3.1 Recognizing and Addressing Childhood Trauma

Childhood trauma can have a profound impact on our adult relationships. The experiences we have during our formative years shape our beliefs, behaviors, and patterns of relating to others. Unresolved childhood trauma can create barriers to building healthy and fulfilling relationships. In this section, we will explore the importance of recognizing and addressing childhood trauma in order to heal and create healthier relationship dynamics.

Understanding Childhood Trauma

Childhood trauma refers to any adverse experiences or events that occur during childhood and have a lasting impact on an individual's emotional, psychological, and social well-being. These experiences can range from physical, emotional, or sexual abuse to neglect, witnessing domestic violence, or experiencing the loss of a loved one. The effects of childhood trauma can be long-lasting and can manifest in various ways, including difficulties in forming and maintaining healthy relationships.

The Impact on Relationships

Childhood trauma can significantly impact our ability to form and maintain healthy relationships. It can create deep-seated fears, insecurities, and trust issues that can hinder our ability to connect with others on an intimate and authentic level. Individuals who have experienced childhood trauma may struggle with feelings of unworthiness, fear of abandonment, or difficulty in expressing emotions. These challenges can lead to patterns of self-sabotage, codependency, or even avoidance of relationships altogether.

Recognizing the Signs

Recognizing the signs of childhood trauma in ourselves and others is an essential step in addressing and healing from its effects. Some common signs and symptoms of unresolved childhood trauma include:

1. Emotional dysregulation: Difficulty managing and expressing emotions, frequent mood swings, or emotional numbness.
2. Trust issues: Difficulty trusting others, fear of intimacy, or a constant need for reassurance.
3. Low self-esteem: Feelings of worthlessness, self-blame, or a persistent sense of shame.
4. Relationship patterns: Repeating unhealthy relationship patterns, such as attracting abusive partners or becoming overly dependent on others.
5. Avoidance: Avoiding emotional intimacy, isolating oneself, or withdrawing from social interactions.
6. Hypervigilance: Being constantly on guard, easily startled, or having a heightened sense of danger.
7. Flashbacks and nightmares: Intrusive memories or nightmares related to past traumatic experiences.
8. Self-destructive behaviors: Engaging in self-harm, substance abuse, or risky behaviors as a way to cope with emotional pain.

Addressing Childhood Trauma

Addressing childhood trauma is a courageous and transformative journey towards healing and creating healthier relationship dynamics. Here are some steps to begin the healing process:

1. Seek professional help: Consider reaching out to a therapist or counselor who specializes in trauma therapy. They can provide guidance, support, and evidence-based techniques to help you navigate the healing process.
2. Educate yourself: Learn about the impact of childhood trauma and how it can affect relationships. Understanding the underlying dynamics can empower you to make positive changes.
3. Practice self-compassion: Be gentle with yourself and acknowledge that healing takes time. Practice self-care activities that promote self-love and self-acceptance.
4. Create a support network: Surround yourself with supportive and understanding individuals who can provide a safe space for you to share your experiences and emotions.
5. Explore trauma-focused therapies: Consider therapies such as Eye Movement Desensitization and Reprocessing (EMDR), Cognitive-Behavioral Therapy (CBT), or somatic experiencing, which can help process and release traumatic memories stored in the body.
6. Engage in self-reflection: Reflect on how your childhood trauma has influenced your beliefs, behaviors, and patterns in relationships. Identify any unhealthy patterns and work towards breaking them.
7. Practice self-care: Engage in activities that promote self-care and self-soothing. This can include exercise, mindfulness, journaling, or engaging in hobbies that bring you joy.
8. Practice healthy boundaries: Learn to set and maintain healthy boundaries in your relationships. This can help protect your emotional well-being and create a sense of safety.
9. Practice forgiveness: Work towards forgiving yourself and others who may have contributed to your childhood trauma. Forgiveness is a

powerful tool for releasing anger, resentment, and moving towards healing.

10. Patience and perseverance: Healing from childhood trauma is a journey that requires patience and perseverance. Be kind to yourself and celebrate small victories along the way.

By recognizing and addressing childhood trauma, we can begin to heal and create healthier relationship dynamics. It is through this healing process that we can cultivate self-love and build real and lasting relationships based on trust, authenticity, and mutual respect. Remember, you are not defined by your past, but you have the power to shape your future.

.2 Processing Grief and Loss

Grief and loss are inevitable parts of life. At some point, we all experience the pain of losing someone or something that is important to us. Whether it is the death of a loved one, the end of a relationship, the loss of a job, or any other significant change, the process of grieving can be challenging and overwhelming.

In this section, we will explore the importance of processing grief and loss in order to heal and move forward in our lives. We will discuss the different stages of grief, strategies for coping with loss, and the role of self-love in the healing process.

Understanding the Stages of Grief

Grief is a complex and individual experience, but it often follows a similar pattern. The renowned psychiatrist Elisabeth Kübler-Ross identified five stages of grief: denial, anger, bargaining, depression, and acceptance. It is important to note that these stages are not linear and can occur in any order. Some individuals may experience all of these stages, while others may only go through a few.

- **Denial**: In the initial stage of grief, it is common to feel a sense of disbelief or denial. We may struggle to accept the reality of the loss and may even try to convince ourselves that it didn't happen.
- **Anger**: As the reality of the loss sets in, anger may arise. We may feel angry at ourselves, at others, or even at the person or situation we have lost. This anger is a natural response to the pain and can be a way of expressing our emotions.
- **Bargaining**: In this stage, we may find ourselves trying to negotiate or make deals in an attempt to reverse the loss. We may make promises to ourselves or a higher power, hoping that it will bring back what we have lost.
- **Depression**: As we begin to fully comprehend the extent of our loss, feelings of sadness and depression may intensify. We may experience a deep sense of emptiness, hopelessness, and a lack of motivation.
- **Acceptance**: The final stage of grief is acceptance. This does not mean that we are necessarily "over" the loss, but rather that we have come to terms with it and are ready to move forward. Acceptance allows us to find meaning and purpose in our lives again.

Coping Strategies for Grief and Loss

While the grieving process is unique to each individual, there are several strategies that can help us navigate through the pain and begin to heal:

1. **Allow yourself to grieve**: It is important to give yourself permission to feel and express your emotions. Suppressing or denying your grief can prolong the healing process. Allow yourself to cry, talk about your feelings, or engage in activities that provide comfort.
2. **Seek support**: Surround yourself with a supportive network of friends, family, or a therapist who can provide a safe space for you to express your emotions. Sharing your grief with others can help alleviate the burden and provide a sense of connection.
3. **Take care of yourself**: During times of grief, it is crucial to prioritize

self-care. This includes getting enough rest, eating nutritious meals, engaging in physical activity, and practicing relaxation techniques such as meditation or deep breathing exercises.

4. **Express your emotions**: Find healthy outlets for your emotions, such as journaling, painting, or engaging in creative activities. Expressing your feelings through art can be a cathartic and healing process.

5. **Create rituals**: Rituals can provide a sense of closure and help us honor the person or thing we have lost. This can include lighting a candle, writing a letter, or creating a memorial in their honor.

6. **Practice self-compassion**: Be gentle with yourself during this difficult time. Understand that grief is a natural response to loss and that it takes time to heal. Treat yourself with kindness, patience, and understanding.

7. **Seek professional help if needed**: If you find that your grief is overwhelming and interfering with your daily life, it may be beneficial to seek professional help. A therapist or counselor can provide guidance and support as you navigate through the grieving process.

The Role of Self-Love in Healing

Self-love plays a crucial role in the healing process of grief and loss. When we practice self-love, we are nurturing ourselves and providing the care and compassion we need during difficult times. Here are some ways in which self-love can support us in processing grief and loss:

1. **Self-compassion**: Self-compassion involves treating ourselves with kindness and understanding. It means acknowledging our pain and suffering without judgment or self-criticism. By practicing self-compassion, we can offer ourselves the same level of care and support that we would offer to a loved one.

2. **Self-care**: Engaging in self-care activities is essential during times of grief. This can include activities that bring us joy, relaxation, and comfort. Taking care of our physical, emotional, and mental well-being allows us to replenish our energy and navigate through the healing

process more effectively.

3. **Setting boundaries**: Grief can be emotionally draining, and it is important to set boundaries with others to protect our emotional well-being. This may involve saying no to additional responsibilities or taking time for ourselves when needed. Setting boundaries allows us to prioritize our healing and self-care.

4. **Honoring our emotions**: Self-love involves honoring and accepting our emotions, even the difficult ones. It is okay to feel anger, sadness, or frustration during the grieving process. By allowing ourselves to fully experience and express these emotions, we can release them and create space for healing.

5. **Practicing self-reflection**: Self-reflection allows us to gain insight into our grief and the lessons it may be teaching us. By taking the time to reflect on our experiences, we can learn and grow from them. This self-reflection can lead to personal growth and a deeper understanding of ourselves.

Remember, healing from grief and loss takes time. Be patient with yourself and trust that with self-love and support, you will gradually find peace and acceptance.

3.3 Empathic Understanding of Ourselves and Others

In the journey of building real and lasting relationships, empathic understanding plays a crucial role. It is an essential step towards healing past wounds and creating a healthy and nurturing environment for ourselves and others. It allows us to let go of resentment, anger, and pain, and opens the door to compassion, understanding, and growth.

The Power of Empathic Understanding

Empathic understanding is not about condoning or forgetting the actions that have caused us harm. It is understanding that people who have harmed us, operate from a place of patterns and behaviors that they learned throughout life. Ourselves and others make choices and decisions based on the personal resources available to us and them at the time. To release ourselves from the burden of carrying negative emotions and to free ourselves from the chains of the past, we can still hold the perpetrator accountable whilst understanding why they behaved the way they did. This releases us from being stuck in a cycle of pain and prevents us from experiencing true happiness and fulfillment in our relationships.

Empathic understanding of ourselves and others is a transformative act of self-love. It allows us to break free from the patterns of blame and victimhood and empowers us to take control of our own emotional well-being. By understand, we create space for healing, growth, and the possibility of rebuilding trust and connection.

Empathic Understand of Ourselves

Often the most challenging form of understanding. We tend to hold ourselves to high standards and can be our own harshest critics. However, it is essential to remember that we are all human, and we make mistakes. Acknowledging our mistakes, taking responsibility for our actions, and learning from them is a vital part of personal growth.

To be empathic towards yourself, start by practicing self-compassion. Treat yourself with kindness and understanding, just as you would a close friend. Recognize that making mistakes is a natural part of the human experience and an opportunity for growth. Allow yourself to learn from your past actions and commit to making positive changes moving forward.

It can also be helpful to engage in self-reflection and identify any underlying beliefs or patterns that may have contributed to the situation. By understanding the root causes of our actions, we can develop greater self-awareness and make conscious choices aligned with our values and intentions.

Remember, empathic understanding is not a one-time event but an ongoing process. Be patient with yourself and practice self-compassion regularly. Celebrate your progress and focus on the person you are becoming rather than dwelling on past mistakes.

Empathic Understanding of Others

This can be equally challenging, especially when the pain they have caused runs deep. Empathic understanding is not about forgiving the other person, but understanding how often the behaviors of others is driven by deep unconscious patterns. It's not about making excuses, but rather explaining the reasons why, while still holding the perpetrator accountable. In doing so, we release their hold over us, and give us the power to move forward.

To begin the process of this, it is important to acknowledge and validate your emotions. Allow yourself to feel the pain, anger, or betrayal that you have experienced. Suppressing or denying these emotions will only prolong the healing process.

Next, try to cultivate an understanding towards the person who has hurt you. This does not mean excusing their behavior or minimizing the impact it had on you. Instead, it involves recognizing that everyone has their own struggles, insecurities, and past wounds, and patterns, that may have influenced their actions.

It can be helpful to put yourself in their shoes and consider the factors that may have contributed to their behavior. This does not justify their actions, but it can provide a broader perspective and help you find compassion and understanding within yourself.

Communication is also key in the process of empathic understanding. If you feel comfortable and safe, express your feelings to the person who has hurt you. Share your perspective and allow them to share theirs. This open dialogue can foster understanding, empathy, and potentially lead to reconciliation.

However, it is important to note that empathic understanding does not always mean reconciliation or maintaining the same level of closeness in the relationship. It's about letting go and creating healthy boundaries to protect yourself from further harm.

The Benefits of Empathic Understanding

1. Emotional Healing: Promotes emotional healing by freeing us from the negative emotions associated with past hurts. It allows us to let go of the pain and move forward with a renewed sense of hope and positivity.
2. Improved Relationships: Can lead to improved relationships by fostering understanding, empathy, and compassion. It creates an opportunity for growth and rebuilding trust, ultimately strengthening the bond between individuals.
3. Reduced Stress and Anxiety: Holding onto grudges and resentment can contribute to increased stress and anxiety. Empathic understanding helps to alleviate these negative emotions, promoting a sense of calm and inner peace.
4. Enhanced Well-being: We let go of the past and focus on the present moment. This shift in perspective allows us to experience greater happiness, contentment, and overall well-being.
5. Personal Growth: It's a powerful catalyst for personal growth and transformation. It challenges us to develop empathy, compassion, and resilience, ultimately leading to a deeper understanding of ourselves and others.

Remember, this is a personal journey, and it may take time. Be patient with yourself and others as you navigate the process. Embrace the healing power of empathic understanding and allow it to guide you towards building real and lasting relationships based on love, compassion, and understanding.

A final word on *empathic understanding*. Anger is a normal emotional feeling that we are often told we shouldn't have. It is perfectly natural to still be angry with those who caused us pain and suffering, and at the same time let go of the resentment and pain that we still feel. Anger gives us the power to release the perpetrator from our emotional lives, whilst still holding them accountable for what they have done.

3.4 Letting Go of Resentment and Toxic Anger

Resentment is a complex and powerful emotion that can have a profound impact on our lives. It is often described as a smoldering fire that burns within us, fueled by feelings of anger, bitterness, and indignation. Resentment can arise from a variety of situations, such as perceived injustices, betrayals, or unmet expectations. It is a deeply ingrained feeling that can be difficult to let go of, and if left unchecked, it can consume us and poison our relationships and overall well-being.

At its core, resentment is a response to feeling wronged or mistreated. It is a natural human reaction to perceived injustices, whether real or imagined. When we experience resentment, we harbor negative emotions towards the person or situation that we believe has caused us harm. These negative emotions can manifest as anger, bitterness, and a desire for revenge or retribution.

Resentment often arises when we feel that our needs, desires, or boundaries have been violated. It can stem from a sense of betrayal, whether it be from a close friend, family member, romantic partner, or even a professional colleague. Resentment can also be directed towards institutions, societal norms, or even ourselves. It is a deeply personal and subjective emotion that can vary in intensity and duration.

One of the defining characteristics of resentment is its persistence. Unlike other emotions that may come and go relatively quickly, resentment has a tendency to linger and fester over time. It can become a chronic state of being, constantly simmering beneath the surface, ready to flare up at the slightest provocation. This prolonged state of resentment can have detrimental effects on our mental, emotional, and even physical well-being.

Resentment can have a profound impact on our relationships. When we hold onto resentment, it can create a barrier between ourselves and others. It can lead to a breakdown in communication, trust, and intimacy. Resentment can also breed a cycle of negativity, where each party becomes increasingly defensive and unwilling to address the underlying issues. Over time, this can erode the foundation of even the strongest relationships.

Furthermore, resentment can have a detrimental effect on our own personal growth and happiness. When we hold onto resentment, we are essentially holding onto the past. It prevents us from fully embracing the present and moving forward in a positive and constructive way. Resentment can consume our thoughts and energy, leaving little room for personal growth, self-reflection, and the pursuit of happiness.

It is important to note that resentment is a normal and natural emotion. It is not inherently good or bad, but rather how we choose to deal with it that determines its impact on our lives. While it is understandable to feel resentment in certain situations, it is crucial to recognize when it becomes unhealthy and detrimental to our well-being.

In the following sections, we will explore the causes of resentment, the effects it can have on our lives, how to recognize it within ourselves, and ultimately, how to break free from its grip. By understanding the nature of resentment and developing strategies to address it, we can begin to heal ourselves and cultivate healthier, more fulfilling relationships.

3.5 Causes of Resentment

Resentment is a complex emotion that can arise from a variety of causes. It is often fueled by feelings of anger, injustice, and betrayal. Understanding the causes of resentment can help us gain insight into why we hold onto these negative emotions and how we can begin to address them.

Unresolved Conflict

One of the primary causes of resentment is unresolved conflict. When conflicts are left unresolved, they can fester and grow, leading to deep-seated resentment. Whether it's a disagreement with a friend, a family member, or a coworker, the longer the conflict remains unresolved, the more resentment can build. This can be particularly true when the conflict involves a breach of trust or a perceived injustice.

Betrayal and Broken Trust

Betrayal and broken trust are significant contributors to resentment. When someone we trust, whether it's a partner, friend, or family member, violates that trust, it can be deeply hurtful. Betrayal can take many forms, such as infidelity, dishonesty, or a breach of confidentiality. These actions can leave us feeling betrayed and resentful, as our expectations of trust and loyalty have been shattered.

Unmet Expectations

Unmet expectations can also lead to resentment. When we have certain expectations of others, whether it's in a personal or professional relationship, and those expectations are not met, it can leave us feeling disappointed and resentful. This can occur when we feel that our needs or desires have been disregarded or when we believe that someone has failed to fulfill their obligations or responsibilities.

Perceived Injustice

Perceived injustice is another common cause of resentment. When we feel that we have been treated unfairly or unjustly, it can ignite feelings of anger and resentment. This can occur in various situations, such as being passed over for a promotion at work, experiencing discrimination, or feeling like we have been treated differently than others in similar circumstances. The sense of injustice can fuel resentment and make it difficult to let go of negative emotions.

Lack of Communication

A lack of communication or poor communication can contribute to the development of resentment. When there is a breakdown in communication, misunderstandings can occur, and conflicts can escalate. Additionally, when individuals fail to express their needs, concerns, or emotions effectively, it can lead to feelings of frustration and resentment. Effective communication is essential in building and maintaining healthy relationships and can help prevent the buildup of resentment.

Unrealistic Expectations

Unrealistic expectations can set the stage for resentment. When we place unrealistic demands on ourselves or others, it can lead to disappointment and frustration. Unrealistic expectations can stem from societal pressures, cultural norms, or personal beliefs. For example, expecting perfection from ourselves or expecting others to always meet our needs and desires can create a breeding ground for resentment when those expectations are not met.

Lack of Boundaries

A lack of boundaries can contribute to resentment in relationships. When we fail to set clear boundaries and assert our needs and limits, it can lead to feelings of resentment. This can occur when we consistently prioritize others' needs over our own or when we allow others to cross our boundaries without consequence. Resentment can build when we feel taken advantage of or when our own well-being is consistently disregarded.

Accumulated Resentment

Resentment can also accumulate over time. When we repeatedly experience situations that cause us pain, anger, or frustration, without effectively addressing or resolving them, the resentment can build up. This can occur in long-term relationships or in situations where there is a pattern of behavior that consistently triggers negative emotions. The accumulation of resentment can make it increasingly challenging to let go and move forward.

In conclusion, resentment can stem from a variety of causes, including unresolved conflict, betrayal, unmet expectations, perceived injustice, lack of communication, unrealistic expectations, lack of boundaries, and accumulated resentment. Understanding these causes can help us identify the roots of our resentment and take steps towards healing and finding resolution. In the next section, we will explore the effects of resentment and how it can impact our well-being and relationships.

3.6 The Effects of Resentment

Resentment is a powerful emotion that can have profound effects on our mental, emotional, and even physical well-being. When we hold onto resentment, it becomes like a fire that keeps burning within us, consuming our thoughts and emotions. It can be a relentless and all-consuming force that affects every aspect of our lives.

One of the most significant effects of resentment is the toll it takes on our mental health. When we harbor resentment, we constantly replay the events or actions that caused us pain or anger. This constant rumination can lead to increased stress, anxiety, and even depression. Our minds become consumed with negative thoughts and emotions, making it difficult to find peace or happiness.

Resentment also has a profound impact on our relationships. When we hold onto resentment, it can create a barrier between ourselves and others. We may become distant, guarded, or even hostile towards the person we resent. This can lead to a breakdown in communication, trust, and intimacy. Resentment can poison even the strongest of relationships, causing irreparable damage if left unchecked.

Furthermore, resentment can also affect our physical health. The stress and negative emotions associated with resentment can manifest in physical symptoms such as headaches, muscle tension, and even chronic pain. Studies have shown that long-term resentment can weaken the immune system, making us more susceptible to illness and disease. It is clear that holding onto resentment not only harms our mental and emotional well-being but also has a detrimental impact on our physical health.

Another effect of resentment is the way it distorts our perception of reality. When we hold onto resentment, we often view the world through a lens of negativity and suspicion. We may become hyper-vigilant, constantly on the lookout for signs of betrayal or mistreatment. This can lead to a cycle of self-fulfilling prophecies, where our negative expectations and behaviors elicit negative responses from others. Our resentment can create a toxic cycle that perpetuates itself, making it difficult to break free from its grip.

Resentment also hinders personal growth and self-improvement. When we are consumed by resentment, our focus becomes fixated on the past and the actions of others. We become stuck in a cycle of blame and victimhood, unable to move forward or take responsibility for our own happiness. Resentment prevents us from learning from our experiences, inhibiting our ability to grow, evolve, and become the best version of ourselves.

Furthermore, resentment can also impact our overall sense of well-being and life satisfaction. When we hold onto resentment, it becomes a heavy burden that weighs us down. It drains our energy, dampens our enthusiasm, and robs us of joy and fulfillment. Resentment keeps us trapped in a negative mindset, preventing us from fully embracing the present moment and finding happiness in our lives.

In conclusion, the effects of resentment are far-reaching and detrimental to our overall well-being. It affects our mental health, relationships, physical health, perception of reality, personal growth, and overall sense of happiness and fulfillment. Holding onto resentment is like carrying a burning fire within us, consuming everything in its path. It is essential to recognize the effects of resentment and take proactive steps to break free from its grip. Only by letting go of resentment can we truly find peace, healing, and happiness in our lives.

3.7 Recognizing Resentment in Yourself

Resentment is a powerful and destructive emotion that can consume us from within. It is often fueled by unresolved anger, hurt, or disappointment towards someone who has wronged us. Recognizing resentment in ourselves is crucial because it allows us to acknowledge and address the negative emotions that are holding us back from living a fulfilling and happy life.

Signs of Resentment

Resentment can manifest in various ways, and it is important to be aware of the signs that indicate its presence in our lives. Here are some common signs that may indicate you are harboring resentment:

1. **Persistent Negative Thoughts**: If you find yourself constantly replaying past events or conversations in your mind, especially those that involve someone who has hurt you, it may be a sign of resentment. These negative thoughts can consume your mental energy and keep you stuck in a cycle of anger and bitterness.

2. **Lack of Empathy**: Resentment can make it difficult to empathize with others, especially those who remind you of the person or situation that caused your resentment. You may find yourself being judgmental or dismissive of their feelings, which can strain your relationships and isolate you from others.

3. **Heightened Emotional Reactivity**: Resentment can make you more sensitive to perceived slights or injustices. You may find yourself reacting strongly to minor incidents or becoming easily triggered by certain words or actions. This heightened emotional reactivity can lead to conflicts and misunderstandings with others.

4. **Avoidance or Withdrawal**: When we resent someone, we may choose to avoid them or withdraw from interactions with them. This can be a subconscious attempt to protect ourselves from further hurt or disappointment. However, avoiding the person or situation that caused

our resentment can also prevent us from finding resolution and healing.

5. **Physical Symptoms**: Resentment can have a profound impact on our physical well-being. It can manifest as headaches, muscle tension, digestive issues, or even chronic pain. These physical symptoms are often a reflection of the emotional turmoil we are experiencing.

The Importance of Self-Reflection

Recognizing resentment in ourselves requires a willingness to engage in self-reflection and introspection. It involves taking an honest look at our emotions, thoughts, and behaviors to identify any underlying resentment that may be present. Self-reflection allows us to gain insight into our own patterns and triggers, helping us to better understand why we feel the way we do.

To begin the process of self-reflection, find a quiet and comfortable space where you can be alone with your thoughts. Take a few deep breaths and allow yourself to relax. Then, ask yourself the following questions:

1. **What events or interactions have caused me to feel anger, hurt, or disappointment?** Reflect on specific situations or relationships that have left a lasting impact on you. Consider the actions or words of others that have contributed to your feelings of resentment.

2. **How has this resentment affected my thoughts and behaviors?** Explore how your resentment has influenced your perception of yourself, others, and the world around you. Consider any negative thought patterns or behaviors that have emerged as a result of your resentment.

3. **Am I holding onto this resentment for a specific reason?** Examine your motivations for holding onto your resentment. Are you seeking validation, justice, or revenge? Understanding your underlying reasons can help you gain clarity and perspective.

4. **What are the consequences of holding onto this resentment?** Consider how your resentment is impacting your overall well-being, relationships, and personal growth. Reflect on whether holding onto

your resentment is serving you or holding you back.

Seeking Support

Recognizing and addressing resentment in ourselves can be a challenging and emotional process. It may be helpful to seek support from trusted friends, family members, or even a therapist. Talking about your feelings with someone who can provide a listening ear and objective perspective can offer valuable insights and guidance.

Additionally, practicing self-care and engaging in activities that bring you joy and relaxation can help alleviate the negative effects of resentment. This may include exercise, meditation, journaling, or pursuing hobbies that promote self-expression and self-discovery.

Remember, recognizing resentment in yourself is the first step towards healing and finding peace. By acknowledging and addressing your resentment, you can begin the journey towards forgiveness, personal growth, and a more fulfilling life.

3.8 Rebuilding Trust in Relationships

Trust is the foundation of any healthy and fulfilling relationship. It is the belief that you can rely on someone, that they have your best interests at heart, and that they will be there for you when you need them. However, trust can be easily broken, and rebuilding it can be a challenging and delicate process. Whether it's a romantic relationship, a friendship, or a professional partnership, rebuilding trust requires time, effort, and open communication.

Understanding the Impact of Broken Trust

When trust is broken in a relationship, it can have a profound impact on both individuals involved. The person who has been betrayed may experience feelings of hurt, anger, and betrayal. They may question their own judgment and struggle with self-doubt. On the other hand, the person who has broken the trust may feel guilt, shame, and remorse for their actions. They may also face the challenge of rebuilding their own self-trust.

Taking Responsibility and Accountability

Rebuilding trust starts with taking responsibility for your actions and being accountable for the harm you have caused. It requires acknowledging the pain you have inflicted on the other person and showing genuine remorse. This means being willing to listen to their feelings and concerns without becoming defensive or dismissive. Taking responsibility also involves making amends and taking steps to prevent similar breaches of trust in the future.

Open and Honest Communication

Effective communication is crucial when rebuilding trust. Both parties need to be willing to engage in open and honest conversations about what happened and how it has affected the relationship. This means actively listening to each other's perspectives, expressing emotions and concerns, and seeking to understand one another's needs and boundaries. It is important to create a safe space where both individuals feel comfortable sharing their thoughts and feelings without fear of judgment or retaliation.

Rebuilding Trust Through Consistency and Reliability

Rebuilding trust requires consistent and reliable behavior over time. It is not enough to apologize and make promises; actions must align with words. This means following through on commitments, being transparent, and demonstrating integrity in all aspects of the relationship. Consistency and reliability help to rebuild trust gradually and allow the injured party to see that the person who broke their trust is committed to change.

Patience and Understanding

Rebuilding trust is a process that takes time, and it is important to be patient and understanding throughout this journey. The person who has been hurt may need time to heal and may have moments of doubt or insecurity. It is crucial to provide reassurance and support, allowing them to express their emotions and concerns without judgment. Patience and understanding also involve recognizing that trust may not be fully restored overnight and that setbacks may occur along the way.

Seeking Professional Help

In some cases, rebuilding trust may require the assistance of a professional, such as a therapist or counselor. A trained professional can provide guidance, support, and tools to navigate the complexities of rebuilding trust. They can help both individuals explore the underlying issues that led to the breach of trust and develop strategies for rebuilding and strengthening the relationship. Seeking professional help can be a valuable investment in the future of the relationship.

Learning from the Past

Rebuilding trust also involves learning from past mistakes and using them as an opportunity for growth and personal development. It requires reflecting on the actions and behaviors that led to the breach of trust and identifying areas for improvement. This may involve addressing personal issues, such as insecurities or unresolved traumas, that may have contributed to the breakdown of trust. By learning from the past, individuals can make conscious efforts to change their behavior and create a healthier and more trusting relationship moving forward.

Celebrating Progress and Growth

As trust is gradually rebuilt, it is important to celebrate the progress and growth that has been made. Acknowledge the efforts and changes that both individuals have made to rebuild trust and express gratitude for the commitment to the relationship. Celebrating milestones along the way can help reinforce the positive changes and create a sense of hope and optimism for the future.

Rebuilding trust in a relationship is a challenging but worthwhile endeavor. It requires patience, understanding, and a commitment to personal growth and change. By taking responsibility, engaging in open communication, and demonstrating consistent and reliable behavior, trust can be rebuilt over time. With forgiveness and a focus on progress and growth, relationships can be transformed into a source of solace and fulfillment.

4

Chapter 4

Creating Healthy Boundaries

4.1 Understanding the Importance of Boundaries

In order to build real and lasting relationships, it is crucial to understand the importance of boundaries. Boundaries are the invisible lines that define where one person ends and another begins. They are the limits we set for ourselves and communicate to others about what is acceptable and what is not in our relationships. Boundaries help us establish a sense of self, maintain our autonomy, and protect our emotional and physical well-being.

The Role of Boundaries in Relationships

Boundaries play a vital role in maintaining healthy relationships. They serve as a framework for how we interact with others and establish the expectations and limits within the relationship. Without clear boundaries, relationships can become chaotic, leading to misunderstandings, conflicts, and emotional distress.

Boundaries help to create a sense of safety and security within relationships. When we have well-defined boundaries, we feel more comfortable expressing our needs, desires, and emotions. This open communication fosters trust and intimacy, as both parties feel heard and respected.

The Benefits of Establishing Boundaries

Establishing and maintaining boundaries in relationships offers numerous benefits. Here are some key advantages:

1. **Self-Respect:** Boundaries demonstrate self-respect and self-worth. By setting boundaries, we communicate to others that we value ourselves and expect to be treated with respect and dignity.
2. **Healthy Communication:** Boundaries encourage open and honest communication. When we clearly express our boundaries, we create an environment where both parties feel safe to express their thoughts and feelings without fear of judgment or rejection.
3. **Emotional Well-being:** Boundaries protect our emotional well-being by preventing others from crossing our limits and causing emotional harm. They help us avoid becoming overwhelmed or drained by others' demands or negative behaviors.
4. **Autonomy and Independence:** Boundaries allow us to maintain our autonomy and independence within relationships. They ensure that we have the freedom to make our own choices, pursue our own interests, and maintain a healthy sense of self.
5. **Respectful Relationships:** Boundaries promote respectful relationships by establishing clear expectations and limits. When both parties understand and respect each other's boundaries, conflicts and misunderstandings are minimized.

Types of Boundaries

Boundaries can be categorized into four main types: physical, emotional, intellectual, and time boundaries. Understanding these different types can help us identify and communicate our boundaries effectively.

1. **Physical Boundaries:** Physical boundaries refer to the physical space we need to feel comfortable and safe. This includes personal space, touch, and physical contact. Physical boundaries can vary from person to person, and it is important to communicate and respect each other's comfort levels.

2. **Emotional Boundaries:** Emotional boundaries involve protecting our emotions and feelings. This includes setting limits on how much emotional support we can provide to others and how much we are willing to share about our own emotions. Emotional boundaries help us maintain a healthy balance between supporting others and taking care of ourselves.

3. **Intellectual Boundaries:** Intellectual boundaries involve respecting each other's thoughts, opinions, and beliefs. It is important to allow space for individual perspectives and avoid imposing our own beliefs on others. Intellectual boundaries foster open-mindedness and encourage healthy discussions.

4. **Time Boundaries:** Time boundaries involve setting limits on how much time we are willing to invest in a relationship or activity. It is important to prioritize our own needs and commitments and communicate our availability to others. Time boundaries help us maintain a healthy work-life balance and prevent burnout.

Communicating and Enforcing Boundaries

Establishing boundaries is only the first step; effectively communicating and enforcing them is equally important. Here are some strategies for communicating and enforcing boundaries in relationships:

1. **Self-Awareness:** Start by understanding your own needs, limits, and values. Reflect on what is important to you and what you are comfortable with in your relationships. This self-awareness will help you establish clear boundaries.

2. **Open Communication:** Clearly and assertively communicate your

boundaries to others. Use "I" statements to express your needs and expectations. Be respectful but firm in your communication, and avoid apologizing for setting boundaries.

3. **Consistency:** Consistently enforce your boundaries. Be firm in maintaining your limits and do not compromise them for the sake of avoiding conflict or pleasing others. Consistency will help others understand and respect your boundaries.

4. **Self-Care:** Prioritize self-care and self-compassion. Taking care of your own needs and well-being is essential for maintaining healthy boundaries. Practice self-care activities that help you recharge and rejuvenate.

5. **Seek Support:** If you are struggling to establish or enforce boundaries, seek support from trusted friends, family, or professionals. They can provide guidance, validation, and encouragement as you navigate the process.

Remember, boundaries are not meant to be rigid walls that isolate us from others. They are healthy guidelines that promote respect, understanding, and mutual growth within relationships. By understanding the importance of boundaries and effectively communicating them, we can create healthier and more fulfilling connections with others.

4.3 Setting Boundaries with Difficult People

Dealing with difficult people can be a challenging and draining experience. Whether it's a toxic friend, a demanding family member, or a manipulative coworker, these individuals can have a significant impact on our emotional well-being and overall happiness. However, it's important to remember that we have the power to set boundaries and protect ourselves from their negative influence.

Understanding Difficult People

Before we delve into setting boundaries, it's crucial to understand the nature of difficult people. These individuals often exhibit certain traits and behaviors that make it challenging to interact with them. Some common characteristics of difficult people include:

1. **Manipulation**: Difficult people often use manipulation tactics to control others and get what they want. They may guilt-trip, gaslight, or play mind games to assert their dominance.
2. **Negativity**: These individuals tend to have a negative outlook on life and often bring others down with their constant complaining, criticism, and pessimism.
3. **Lack of empathy**: Difficult people often struggle to understand or consider the feelings and perspectives of others. They may be self-centered and dismissive of others' emotions.
4. **Boundary violations**: Difficult people often have little respect for personal boundaries and may invade your space, both physically and emotionally.
5. **Conflict-prone**: These individuals may thrive on conflict and drama, constantly seeking out arguments and disagreements.

The Importance of Setting Boundaries

Setting boundaries with difficult people is essential for maintaining your mental and emotional well-being. Without clear boundaries, you may find yourself constantly drained, stressed, and overwhelmed by their behavior. By establishing and enforcing boundaries, you can protect yourself from their negative influence and create a healthier dynamic in your relationships.

Steps to Setting Boundaries with Difficult People

1. **Identify your boundaries**: Before you can communicate your boundaries to others, it's crucial to identify them for yourself. Reflect on what behaviors and actions are unacceptable to you and determine where you need to draw the line.

2. **Communicate assertively**: When setting boundaries, it's important to communicate assertively and clearly. Use "I" statements to express how their behavior affects you and what you need from them. For example, instead of saying, "You always make me feel guilty," say, "I feel guilty when you say certain things."

3. **Be consistent**: Consistency is key when it comes to setting boundaries. Stick to your boundaries and enforce them consistently. If you allow someone to cross your boundaries occasionally, they may not take them seriously.

4. **Practice self-care**: Dealing with difficult people can be emotionally draining. Make sure to prioritize self-care and engage in activities that recharge and rejuvenate you. Taking care of yourself will give you the strength and resilience to maintain your boundaries.

5. **Seek support**: It can be helpful to seek support from trusted friends, family members, or even a therapist. They can provide guidance, validation, and encouragement as you navigate setting boundaries with difficult people.

6. **Consider consequences**: Setting boundaries may come with consequences, especially if the difficult person is resistant to change. Be prepared for potential pushback or negative reactions. Remember that you have the right to prioritize your well-being and that their reactions are not your responsibility.

7. **Reevaluate the relationship**: In some cases, setting boundaries may not be enough to maintain a healthy relationship with a difficult person. If their behavior continues to negatively impact your well-being despite your efforts, it may be necessary to reevaluate the relationship and consider distancing yourself or even ending the relationship altogether.

Examples of Setting Boundaries with Difficult People

1. **Boundary: Emotional Manipulation**

- "I will not engage in conversations where you try to manipulate or guilt-trip me."
- "If you continue to use emotional manipulation, I will need to take a break from our relationship."

1. **Boundary: Disrespectful Language**

- "I expect to be spoken to with respect. If you use derogatory language towards me, I will end the conversation."
- "If you cannot communicate without resorting to insults, I will not engage in further discussions."

1. **Boundary: Invasion of Personal Space**

- "I need you to respect my personal space. Please do not touch me without my consent."
- "If you continue to invade my personal space, I will need to limit our interactions."

Remember, setting boundaries is not about controlling or changing the other person. It's about taking care of yourself and creating a healthier dynamic in your relationships. By setting and maintaining boundaries with difficult people, you can protect your well-being and foster healthier and more fulfilling connections.

4.4 Maintaining Boundaries in Intimate Relationships

Intimate relationships have the potential to bring us immense joy, love, and fulfillment. However, they can also be a source of conflict, frustration, and even pain. One of the key factors in creating and sustaining a healthy intimate relationship is the establishment and maintenance of boundaries.

Boundaries are the invisible lines that define where we end and others begin. They are essential for maintaining our sense of self, autonomy, and emotional well-being within a relationship. When boundaries are not respected or are unclear, it can lead to a variety of issues such as codependency, resentment, and a loss of personal identity.

In intimate relationships, it is crucial to establish and communicate boundaries from the beginning. This allows both partners to understand each other's needs, expectations, and limits. Here are some strategies for maintaining boundaries in intimate relationships:

1. Self-Awareness and Reflection

Before you can effectively communicate your boundaries to your partner, it is essential to have a clear understanding of your own needs, values, and limits. Take the time to reflect on what is important to you in a relationship and what behaviors or actions are unacceptable. This self-awareness will provide a solid foundation for establishing and maintaining boundaries.

2. Open and Honest Communication

Effective communication is key to maintaining boundaries in any relationship. Clearly and assertively express your needs, desires, and limits to your partner. Use "I" statements to express how certain behaviors or actions make you feel and explain why they are important to you. Encourage your partner to do the same, and actively listen to their needs and boundaries as well.

3. Consistency and Follow-Through

Establishing boundaries is only the first step; it is equally important to consistently enforce them. Be firm and consistent in upholding your boundaries, even when it may be challenging or uncomfortable. This sends a clear message to your partner that your boundaries are non-negotiable and deserve respect.

4. Respect for Individual Autonomy

In a healthy intimate relationship, both partners should have the freedom to pursue their individual interests, goals, and friendships. Encourage and support your partner's autonomy, and ensure that you maintain your own as well. Avoid becoming overly dependent on each other for happiness and fulfillment, as this can lead to a loss of personal boundaries.

5. Regular Check-Ins

As individuals grow and change, so do their boundaries. It is important to regularly check in with yourself and your partner to ensure that your boundaries are still aligned and being respected. Discuss any changes or adjustments that may be necessary and be open to renegotiating boundaries as needed.

6. Seek Professional Help if Needed

If you find that maintaining boundaries in your intimate relationship is consistently challenging or causing significant distress, it may be beneficial to seek the guidance of a professional therapist or counselor. They can provide you with the tools and support needed to navigate and address any underlying issues that may be impacting your ability to maintain healthy boundaries.

7. Practice Self-Care

Maintaining boundaries in intimate relationships requires self-care and self-love. Take the time to prioritize your own well-being and engage in activities that bring you joy and fulfillment. Nurture your own emotional, physical, and mental health, as this will strengthen your ability to maintain boundaries and contribute to a healthy relationship.

8. Mutual Respect and Understanding

Remember that maintaining boundaries is a two-way street. It is important to respect and understand your partner's boundaries just as much as you expect them to respect yours. Foster an environment of mutual respect, empathy, and understanding, where both partners feel safe and supported in expressing their needs and limits.

In conclusion, maintaining boundaries in intimate relationships is crucial for fostering a healthy and fulfilling connection. By cultivating self-awareness, practicing open communication, and consistently upholding boundaries, you can create a relationship that is built on mutual respect, understanding, and love. Remember that boundaries are not meant to restrict or control, but rather to create a space where both partners can thrive as individuals while nurturing their connection.

5

Chapter 5

Effective Communication Strategies

5.1 Active Listening and Empathy

In order to build real and lasting relationships, it is essential to develop effective communication strategies. One of the most important skills in this regard is active listening and empathy. Active listening involves fully engaging with the speaker, not just hearing their words but also understanding their emotions and intentions. Empathy, on the other hand, is the ability to put yourself in someone else's shoes and understand their perspective.

Active listening and empathy are crucial components of healthy communication because they create a safe and supportive environment for open and honest dialogue. When we actively listen to others, we show them that we value their thoughts and feelings, which in turn fosters trust and deepens the connection between individuals. By practicing empathy, we demonstrate that we genuinely care about the other person's experiences and emotions, leading to greater understanding and compassion.

To become an active listener, it is important to focus on the speaker and give them your full attention. This means putting aside distractions such as phones or other devices and truly being present in the conversation. Maintain eye contact, nod or provide other non-verbal cues to show that you are engaged

57

and interested in what the speaker is saying. Avoid interrupting or interjecting with your own thoughts or opinions, as this can derail the conversation and make the speaker feel unheard.

Another key aspect of active listening is reflecting back what the speaker has said. This can be done by paraphrasing or summarizing their words to ensure that you have understood their message correctly. This not only helps to clarify any misunderstandings but also shows the speaker that you are actively listening and trying to comprehend their perspective. Additionally, asking open-ended questions can encourage the speaker to elaborate on their thoughts and feelings, further deepening the conversation.

Empathy goes hand in hand with active listening. It involves not only understanding the speaker's words but also their emotions and experiences. To practice empathy, try to imagine yourself in the other person's situation and consider how you would feel if you were in their shoes. This requires setting aside your own biases and judgments and truly trying to understand the other person's point of view. By showing empathy, you validate the other person's emotions and create a space where they feel safe to express themselves fully.

It is important to note that active listening and empathy are not about agreeing with everything the speaker says or trying to solve their problems. Instead, they are about creating a supportive and non-judgmental space where the speaker feels heard and understood. This can be particularly valuable in times of conflict or disagreement, as active listening and empathy can help to de-escalate tension and foster a sense of mutual respect.

By practicing active listening and empathy, we can strengthen our relationships and build a foundation of trust and understanding. When we truly listen to others and empathize with their experiences, we create a space for open and honest communication. This allows for the resolution of conflicts, the sharing of vulnerabilities, and the deepening of emotional connections.

In addition to benefiting our relationships with others, active listening and empathy also have a positive impact on our own well-being. When we actively listen to others and show empathy, we cultivate a sense of compassion and understanding within ourselves. This not only enhances our ability to connect with others but also promotes self-growth and personal development.

In conclusion, active listening and empathy are essential skills for building real and lasting relationships. By fully engaging with others, understanding their perspectives, and validating their emotions, we create a safe and supportive environment for open and honest communication. Through active listening and empathy, we can foster trust, deepen connections, and promote personal growth both within ourselves and in our relationships with others.

5.2 Expressing Needs and Desires

In any relationship, it is essential to express your needs and desires effectively. However, many people struggle with this aspect of communication, often leading to misunderstandings, unmet expectations, and frustration. Expressing your needs and desires openly and honestly is crucial for building real and lasting relationships. It allows both parties to understand each other's wants and work towards meeting them. In this section, we will explore effective strategies for expressing your needs and desires in a healthy and constructive manner.

The Importance of Self-Awareness

Before you can effectively express your needs and desires to others, it is crucial to have a clear understanding of what they are. This requires self-awareness and introspection. Take the time to reflect on your own wants and needs in the relationship. What are the things that are important to you? What do you value? Understanding your own desires will help you communicate them more effectively to others.

Use "I" Statements

When expressing your needs and desires, it is important to use "I" statements rather than "you" statements. "I" statements focus on your own feelings and experiences, which can help prevent the other person from becoming defensive or feeling attacked. For example, instead of saying, "You never listen to me," you can say, "I feel unheard when I don't feel like you're actively listening to me." This approach allows you to express your needs without placing blame on the other person.

Be Clear and Specific

When expressing your needs and desires, it is essential to be clear and specific. Vague or ambiguous statements can lead to confusion and misinterpretation. Clearly articulate what you want or need from the other person, providing specific examples if necessary. For instance, instead of saying, "I want more support," you can say, "I would appreciate it if you could offer to help with household chores more often."

Choose the Right Time and Place

Timing and environment play a significant role in effective communication. Choose a time and place where both parties can focus and engage in a meaningful conversation. Avoid discussing important matters when either of you is stressed, tired, or distracted. Create a safe and comfortable space where both parties can express themselves without fear of judgment or interruption.

Active Listening

Expressing your needs and desires is not a one-way street. It is equally important to listen actively to the other person's response. Give them your full attention, maintain eye contact, and show genuine interest in what they have to say. Reflect back on their words to ensure you understand their perspective correctly. Active listening fosters understanding and empathy, creating a space for open and honest communication.

Practice Empathy and Understanding

When expressing your needs and desires, it is crucial to approach the conversation with empathy and understanding. Recognize that the other person may have their own needs and desires, which may differ from yours. Be open to their perspective and willing to find a compromise that meets both parties' needs. Empathy and understanding create a foundation of trust and respect in the relationship.

Avoid Making Assumptions

Assumptions can be detrimental to effective communication. Instead of assuming what the other person wants or needs, ask for clarification. Avoid making assumptions based on past experiences or preconceived notions. Give the other person an opportunity to express themselves fully and provide the necessary information for you to understand their perspective accurately.

Practice Active Problem-Solving

Expressing your needs and desires often involves problem-solving. If there are obstacles or challenges preventing your needs from being met, work together with the other person to find solutions. Brainstorm ideas, consider different perspectives, and be open to compromise. Active problem-solving strengthens the relationship and demonstrates a willingness to work together towards a common goal.

Seek Professional Help if Needed

Sometimes, expressing your needs and desires can be challenging, especially if there are underlying issues or unresolved conflicts in the relationship. In such cases, seeking professional help, such as couples therapy or relationship counseling, can be beneficial. A trained therapist can provide guidance and support in navigating difficult conversations and finding healthy ways to express your needs and desires.

Practice Patience and Persistence

Effective communication takes practice and patience. It may take time for both parties to fully understand and meet each other's needs and desires. Be patient with yourself and the other person as you navigate this process. Keep the lines of communication open and continue to express your needs and desires in a constructive and respectful manner. With persistence and commitment, you can build a relationship where both parties feel heard, understood, and valued.

Expressing your needs and desires is an essential aspect of building real and lasting relationships. By cultivating self-awareness, using "I" statements, being clear and specific, choosing the right time and place, practicing active listening and empathy, avoiding assumptions, engaging in active problem-solving, seeking professional help if needed, and practicing patience and persistence, you can create a foundation of open and honest communication. When both parties feel comfortable expressing their needs and desires, the relationship can thrive, leading to greater satisfaction and fulfillment for all involved.

5.3 Resolving Conflict Constructively

Conflict is an inevitable part of any relationship. Whether it's a romantic partnership, a familial bond, a friendship, or a professional connection, disagreements and clashes of opinions are bound to occur. However, it's not the presence of conflict that determines the health of a relationship, but rather how it is resolved. Resolving conflict constructively is essential for building and maintaining real and lasting relationships.

Understanding Conflict

Before delving into strategies for resolving conflict, it's important to understand the nature of conflict itself. Conflict arises when there is a perceived or actual difference in needs, desires, or perspectives between individuals. It can stem from misunderstandings, unmet expectations, differing values, or even external factors that impact the relationship.

Conflict can manifest in various ways, ranging from minor disagreements to intense arguments. It can be overt or subtle, and it can occur in both verbal and non-verbal forms. Regardless of the form it takes, conflict can be emotionally charged and have a significant impact on the individuals involved.

The Importance of Constructive Conflict Resolution

Resolving conflict constructively is crucial for the overall health and well-being of a relationship. When conflict is left unresolved or is handled in a destructive manner, it can lead to resentment, distance, and even the breakdown of the relationship itself. On the other hand, when conflict is addressed in a constructive manner, it can strengthen the bond between individuals, foster understanding, and promote growth and intimacy.

Constructive conflict resolution allows individuals to express their needs and concerns openly and honestly while also actively listening to the other person's perspective. It involves finding common ground, seeking compromise, and working together to find mutually beneficial solutions. By resolving conflict constructively, individuals can build trust, deepen their connection, and create a safe and supportive environment for both parties.

Strategies for Resolving Conflict Constructively

1. **Maintain Calm and Emotional Regulation:** When conflict arises, it's important to remain calm and composed. Emotions can run high during disagreements, but reacting impulsively or aggressively can escalate the situation further. Take a moment to breathe, collect your thoughts, and regulate your emotions before engaging in the resolution process.

2. **Practice Active Listening:** Active listening is a fundamental skill in conflict resolution. It involves giving your full attention to the other person, seeking to understand their perspective without interrupting or judging. Show empathy and validate their feelings, even if you don't agree with their point of view. This creates a safe space for open and honest communication.

3. **Use "I" Statements:** When expressing your own needs and concerns, use "I" statements instead of "you" statements. For cxample, say "I feel hurt when this happens" instead of "You always do this." This approach avoids blaming and accusatory language, which can escalate conflict. Focus on expressing your own emotions and experiences rather than attacking the other person.

4. **Seek to Understand:** Take the time to understand the underlying reasons behind the conflict. Ask open-ended questions to gain insight into the other person's perspective and motivations. This helps to foster empathy and can lead to a deeper understanding of each other's needs and desires.

5. **Find Common Ground:** Look for areas of agreement or shared goals. Identifying common ground can help shift the focus from the conflict itself to finding solutions that benefit both parties. By emphasizing shared interests, you can work together towards a resolution that satisfies both individuals.

6. **Brainstorm Solutions:** Once you have a clear understanding of each other's perspectives, brainstorm potential solutions together. Encourage creativity and open-mindedness. Consider multiple options and evaluate their feasibility and potential outcomes. Aim for win-

win solutions that address the needs and concerns of both individuals involved.

7. **Practice Compromise:** In some cases, finding a middle ground or compromising may be necessary. This involves each person giving up something in order to reach a resolution. Compromise should be a mutual decision and not one-sided. It's important to ensure that both individuals feel heard and that their needs are being considered.

8. **Communicate Boundaries:** Conflict resolution is an opportunity to establish or reinforce boundaries within the relationship. Clearly communicate your boundaries and expectations, and be receptive to the other person's boundaries as well. This helps to prevent future conflicts and promotes a healthier dynamic moving forward.

9. **Seek Mediation if Needed:** In certain situations, seeking the help of a neutral third party can be beneficial. A mediator, such as a therapist or counselor, can provide guidance and facilitate productive communication. They can help navigate complex conflicts and provide a fresh perspective on the situation.

10. **Learn from the Conflict:** Conflict can be an opportunity for growth and learning. Reflect on the conflict and the resolution process. Consider what you have learned about yourself, the other person, and the relationship as a whole. Use this knowledge to strengthen the relationship and prevent similar conflicts in the future.

Resolving conflict constructively requires patience, empathy, and a willingness to work towards a mutually beneficial resolution. It's important to remember that conflict is a natural part of any relationship, and it can be an opportunity for growth and deeper understanding. By approaching conflict with a constructive mindset, individuals can build stronger, more resilient relationships based on trust, respect, and effective communication.

5.4 Navigating Difficult Conversations

Difficult conversations are an inevitable part of any relationship. Whether it's addressing a sensitive topic, expressing a disagreement, or discussing a challenging issue, these conversations can often be uncomfortable and emotionally charged. However, learning how to navigate difficult conversations is crucial for building real and lasting relationships. It allows for open communication, understanding, and growth within the relationship. In this section, we will explore strategies to effectively navigate difficult conversations and foster healthier connections.

Understanding the Importance of Difficult Conversations

Difficult conversations are not something to be avoided or feared. In fact, they are essential for the growth and development of any relationship. These conversations provide an opportunity to address underlying issues, express needs and desires, and work towards finding mutually beneficial solutions. By avoiding difficult conversations, we risk allowing resentment, misunderstandings, and unresolved conflicts to fester, ultimately damaging the relationship.

Cultivating a Safe and Supportive Environment

Creating a safe and supportive environment is crucial when engaging in difficult conversations. Both parties should feel comfortable expressing their thoughts and emotions without fear of judgment or retaliation. Here are some strategies to foster a safe space:

1. Active Listening: Practice active listening by giving your full attention to the speaker. Maintain eye contact, nod to show understanding, and avoid interrupting. This demonstrates respect and validates the speaker's feelings.
2. Empathy and Understanding: Put yourself in the other person's shoes

and try to understand their perspective. Show empathy by acknowledging their emotions and validating their experiences. This helps to create a sense of connection and mutual understanding.

3. Non-Verbal Cues: Pay attention to your body language and non-verbal cues. Maintain an open posture, avoid crossing your arms, and use facial expressions that convey attentiveness and empathy. These non-verbal cues can help to establish trust and openness during the conversation.

4. Use "I" Statements: When expressing your thoughts and feelings, use "I" statements instead of "you" statements. For example, say "I feel hurt when…" instead of "You always make me feel…" This approach takes ownership of your emotions and avoids blaming the other person, fostering a more constructive conversation.

Setting the Stage for Productive Conversations

Before engaging in a difficult conversation, it's important to set the stage for a productive dialogue. Here are some steps to consider:

1. Choose the Right Time and Place: Find a time and place where both parties can focus and have privacy. Avoid having difficult conversations in public or when either person is feeling stressed or distracted.

2. Clarify Your Intentions: Clearly communicate your intentions for the conversation. Let the other person know that your goal is to address the issue and find a resolution that benefits both parties. This helps to create a sense of purpose and collaboration.

3. Stay Calm and Manage Emotions: Difficult conversations can evoke strong emotions. It's important to stay calm and manage your emotions during the conversation. Take deep breaths, practice mindfulness, and remind yourself of the importance of maintaining a respectful and constructive dialogue.

Effective Communication Strategies

Effective communication is key to navigating difficult conversations successfully. Here are some strategies to enhance communication during challenging discussions:

1. Use Active Listening: Practice active listening by fully focusing on the speaker's words and non-verbal cues. Avoid interrupting and ask clarifying questions to ensure you understand their perspective.
2. Reflect and Validate: Reflect back what the speaker has said to show that you understand their point of view. Validate their feelings and experiences, even if you don't agree with them. This helps to create a sense of empathy and fosters a more open and understanding conversation.
3. Speak Clearly and Respectfully: Use clear and concise language to express your thoughts and feelings. Avoid using accusatory or inflammatory language that may escalate the situation. Be respectful and mindful of your tone of voice and body language.
4. Seek Common Ground: Look for areas of agreement or common ground to build upon. Finding shared values or goals can help to bridge the gap and create a more collaborative conversation.

Managing Conflict and Finding Solutions

Difficult conversations often involve addressing conflicts or disagreements. Here are some strategies to manage conflict and work towards finding solutions:

1. Focus on the Issue, Not the Person: Keep the conversation focused on the specific issue at hand and avoid personal attacks or criticism. Separate the behavior from the person and address the problem constructively.
2. Brainstorm Solutions: Encourage both parties to brainstorm potential solutions to the issue. Be open to different perspectives and ideas. This collaborative approach helps to foster a sense of ownership and

commitment to finding a resolution.

3. Compromise and Flexibility: Be willing to compromise and find middle ground. Understand that finding a solution may require both parties to make concessions. Flexibility and a willingness to find a win-win outcome can help to resolve conflicts more effectively.

4. Seek Professional Help if Needed: In some cases, difficult conversations may require the assistance of a mediator or therapist. If the conversation becomes too challenging or unproductive, consider seeking professional help to facilitate the dialogue and find a resolution.

Navigating difficult conversations is a skill that can be developed with practice and patience. By creating a safe and supportive environment, setting the stage for productive conversations, and employing effective communication strategies, you can foster healthier and more fulfilling relationships. Remember, difficult conversations are an opportunity for growth and understanding, leading to stronger and more authentic connections.

6

Chapter 6

Building Trust and Intimacy

6.1 Creating Emotional Safety

In order to build real and lasting relationships, it is essential to create emotional safety within the connection. Emotional safety refers to an environment where individuals feel secure, supported, and accepted in expressing their thoughts, feelings, and vulnerabilities without fear of judgment or rejection. When emotional safety is present, it fosters trust, intimacy, and open communication, allowing relationships to thrive.

The Importance of Emotional Safety

Emotional safety is the foundation upon which healthy relationships are built. It provides a sense of stability and security, allowing individuals to be their authentic selves and share their true emotions without reservation. When emotional safety is lacking, relationships can become strained, leading to misunderstandings, conflicts, and a breakdown in trust.

Creating emotional safety is particularly crucial in intimate relationships, where vulnerability and deep emotional connection are essential. However, it is equally important in all types of relationships, including friendships, family connections, and even professional relationships. When emotional safety is established, it creates an environment where individuals can grow, heal, and flourish together.

Building Emotional Safety

Creating emotional safety requires intentional effort and a commitment to nurturing the relationship. Here are some strategies to help foster emotional safety:

1. Active Listening and Validation

One of the fundamental ways to create emotional safety is through active listening and validation. When someone shares their thoughts or feelings, it is important to give them your full attention, maintain eye contact, and show genuine interest. Reflecting back what they have said and validating their emotions helps them feel heard and understood, strengthening the emotional bond between you.

2. Non-Judgmental Attitude

To create emotional safety, it is crucial to adopt a non-judgmental attitude. Avoid criticizing or belittling the other person's thoughts, feelings, or experiences. Instead, strive to be accepting and empathetic, recognizing that everyone's perspective is valid. This encourages open and honest communication, allowing both individuals to feel safe expressing themselves without fear of judgment.

3. Trust and Reliability

Trust is a vital component of emotional safety. Building trust involves being reliable and consistent in your actions and words. Follow through on your commitments, be honest and transparent, and maintain confidentiality when necessary. By demonstrating trustworthiness, you create an environment where individuals feel secure and confident in sharing their innermost thoughts and feelings.

4. Boundaries and Respect

Respecting personal boundaries is essential for emotional safety. Each individual has their own limits and comfort zones, and it is important to honor and respect them. Communicate openly about boundaries and ensure that they are mutually understood and respected. Respecting boundaries fosters a sense of safety and allows individuals to feel in control of their own emotional well-being within the relationship.

5. Conflict Resolution

Conflict is inevitable in any relationship, but how it is handled can greatly impact emotional safety. Encourage open and respectful communication during conflicts, allowing both parties to express their perspectives without fear of retaliation. Focus on finding solutions rather than placing blame, and strive for compromise and understanding. By resolving conflicts in a healthy and constructive manner, emotional safety is preserved, and the relationship can grow stronger.

6. Emotional Support

Providing emotional support is a crucial aspect of creating emotional safety. Be there for the other person during challenging times, offering empathy, compassion, and understanding. Validate their emotions and provide a safe space for them to express their feelings without judgment. By offering emotional support, you create an environment where individuals feel valued and cared for, strengthening the emotional bond between you.

7. Self-Awareness and Self-Reflection

Creating emotional safety also requires self-awareness and self-reflection. Take the time to understand your own emotions, triggers, and patterns of behavior that may impact the relationship. Be willing to acknowledge and address any personal issues or unresolved traumas that may hinder emotional safety. By working on your own emotional well-being, you contribute to a healthier and safer relationship dynamic.

The Benefits of Emotional Safety

When emotional safety is established within a relationship, it brings forth numerous benefits:

• Trust and intimacy: Emotional safety fosters trust, allowing individuals to open up and be vulnerable with one another. This deepens the emotional connection and strengthens the bond between individuals.

- Effective communication: When individuals feel emotionally safe, they are more likely to communicate openly and honestly. This leads to better understanding, reduced misunderstandings, and improved conflict resolution.
- Personal growth: Emotional safety provides a supportive environment for personal growth and self-discovery. Individuals feel encouraged to explore their true selves, express their needs and desires, and pursue their goals and aspirations.
- Reduced anxiety and stress: Emotional safety reduces anxiety and stress within the relationship. When individuals feel secure and accepted, they can relax and be themselves, leading to a more harmonious and peaceful connection.
- Increased happiness and satisfaction: Emotional safety contributes to overall happiness and satisfaction within the relationship. When individuals feel safe and supported, they experience greater joy, fulfillment, and contentment in their connection.

By prioritizing emotional safety and implementing strategies to foster it, individuals can create a solid foundation for healthy and fulfilling relationships. When emotional safety is present, relationships can flourish, allowing individuals to experience the true depth and beauty of human connection.

6.2 Developing Trust in Relationships

Trust is the foundation of any healthy and lasting relationship. It is the belief that you can rely on someone, that they have your best interests at heart, and that they will be there for you when you need them. Developing trust in relationships is essential for creating a strong bond and fostering a sense of security and intimacy.

Understanding Trust

Trust is not something that can be built overnight. It takes time, effort, and consistent behavior to develop trust in a relationship. Trust is built through a series of interactions and experiences that demonstrate reliability, honesty, and integrity. It is a delicate balance that requires both parties to be open, vulnerable, and willing to invest in the relationship.

Building Trust

1. **Open and Honest Communication:** Effective communication is crucial for building trust in any relationship. It is important to be open and honest with each other, sharing your thoughts, feelings, and concerns. Clear and transparent communication helps to establish a sense of trust and understanding.
2. **Consistency:** Consistency is key when it comes to building trust. It is important to follow through on your commitments and promises. Being consistent in your words and actions helps to create a sense of reliability and dependability, which are essential for trust to flourish.
3. **Reliability:** Being reliable means being there for the other person when they need you. It involves being consistent in your actions and showing up for the relationship. Reliability builds trust by demonstrating that you can be counted on and that you value the relationship.
4. **Respect and Empathy:** Trust is also built through mutual respect and empathy. It is important to listen to each other's perspectives, validate each other's feelings, and show understanding and compassion. Respecting each other's boundaries and treating each other with kindness and empathy helps to foster trust.
5. **Accountability:** Taking responsibility for your actions and being accountable for your mistakes is crucial for building trust. When you make a mistake, own up to it, apologize sincerely, and take steps to make amends. Being accountable shows that you are committed to the relationship and willing to learn and grow from your experiences.

6. **Building Trust in Small Steps:** Trust is not built overnight. It is a gradual process that requires patience and understanding. Start by building trust in small steps, gradually increasing the level of vulnerability and openness in the relationship. Celebrate the small victories and acknowledge the progress made along the way.

Rebuilding Trust

Trust can be fragile, and sometimes it may be broken due to a breach of trust or betrayal. Rebuilding trust requires time, effort, and a commitment to change. Here are some steps to help rebuild trust in a relationship:

1. **Acknowledge the Hurt:** It is important to acknowledge the pain and hurt caused by the breach of trust. Both parties need to be willing to confront the issue and have an open and honest conversation about what happened.
2. **Take Responsibility:** The person who broke the trust needs to take responsibility for their actions. They should apologize sincerely, express remorse, and show a genuine commitment to change their behavior.
3. **Rebuilding Transparency:** Rebuilding trust requires transparency and openness. Both parties should be willing to share their thoughts, feelings, and concerns. This includes being open about past mistakes and working together to establish new boundaries and expectations.
4. **Consistency and Reliability:** Rebuilding trust requires consistent and reliable behavior. The person who broke the trust needs to demonstrate through their actions that they can be trusted again. This involves following through on commitments, being reliable, and showing up for the relationship.
5. **Seeking Professional Help:** In some cases, rebuilding trust may require the assistance of a therapist or counselor. A professional can provide guidance, support, and tools to help navigate the process of rebuilding trust.

Remember, rebuilding trust takes time and patience. It is important to be realistic and understand that trust may not be fully restored overnight. However, with commitment, effort, and a willingness to change, it is possible to rebuild trust and strengthen the relationship.

Trust and Self-Love

Developing trust in relationships is closely intertwined with self-love. When you have a healthy sense of self-love, you are more likely to trust yourself and others. Self-love allows you to set boundaries, communicate effectively, and make choices that align with your values and needs.

To develop trust in relationships, it is important to cultivate self-love by:

1. **Building Self-Esteem:** Developing a positive self-image and recognizing your worth is essential for building trust. When you have a strong sense of self-esteem, you are more likely to trust yourself and others.
2. **Practicing Self-Compassion:** Being kind and compassionate towards yourself allows you to be more understanding and forgiving towards others. Self-compassion helps to create a safe and nurturing environment for trust to thrive.
3. **Honoring Your Boundaries:** Setting and maintaining healthy boundaries is crucial for developing trust. When you honor your boundaries, you communicate to others what is acceptable and what is not, creating a foundation of trust and respect.
4. **Listening to Your Intuition:** Trusting your intuition and inner wisdom is an important aspect of self-love. When you listen to your gut instincts, you are more likely to make choices that align with your values and protect your well-being.

By cultivating self-love, you not only enhance your own well-being but also create a solid foundation for trust and intimacy in your relationships.

In conclusion, developing trust in relationships is a gradual process that requires open and honest communication, consistency, reliability, respect, empathy, and accountability. Rebuilding trust after a breach requires acknowledging the hurt, taking responsibility, rebuilding transparency, and demonstrating consistent and reliable behavior. Trust is closely connected to self-love, and cultivating self-love is essential for developing trust in relationships. By building self-esteem, practicing self-compassion, honoring boundaries, and listening to your intuition, you can create a strong foundation of trust and foster healthy and lasting relationships.

6.3 Enhancing Intimacy and Connection

In our closest relationships, we often find ourselves yearning for a deeper sense of intimacy and connection. Whether it's with a romantic partner, a parent, a child, a friend, or a colleague, we may feel a sense of crisis rather than solace in these relationships. We desire change, but it seems that nothing we do can bring about the transformation we seek.

Enhancing intimacy and connection requires a willingness to explore and understand the dynamics at play within our relationships. It involves a commitment to personal growth and a willingness to communicate openly and honestly with our loved ones. By taking intentional steps to enhance intimacy and connection, we can create a foundation of trust and understanding that can transform our relationships into sources of comfort and support.

The Importance of Emotional Availability

One of the key factors in enhancing intimacy and connection is emotional availability. Being emotionally available means being present and attuned to the emotions and needs of our loved ones. It requires us to be open and vulnerable, willing to share our own emotions and experiences, and to listen with empathy and understanding.

To enhance emotional availability, it's important to cultivate self-awareness and emotional intelligence. This involves recognizing and understanding our own emotions, as well as being able to empathize with the emotions of others.

By developing these skills, we can create a safe space for open and honest communication, which is essential for building intimacy and connection.

Cultivating Trust and Vulnerability

Trust is the foundation of any intimate relationship. Without trust, it's difficult to truly connect with another person on a deep level. Building trust requires consistency, reliability, and honesty. It also involves being vulnerable and allowing ourselves to be seen and known by our loved ones.

To cultivate trust, it's important to communicate openly and honestly. This means expressing our thoughts, feelings, and needs in a clear and respectful manner. It also involves actively listening to our loved ones and validating their experiences. By creating a safe and non-judgmental space for communication, we can foster trust and deepen our connection.

Vulnerability is closely linked to trust. It involves allowing ourselves to be seen and known, even when it feels uncomfortable or scary. By embracing vulnerability, we can create opportunities for deeper emotional connection and understanding. This may involve sharing our fears, insecurities, and past experiences with our loved ones. When we are vulnerable, we invite our loved ones to do the same, creating a space for mutual growth and support.

Building Emotional Intimacy

Emotional intimacy is the ability to share our deepest thoughts, feelings, and desires with another person. It involves a sense of trust, understanding, and acceptance. Building emotional intimacy requires ongoing effort and commitment from both partners.

To enhance emotional intimacy, it's important to create dedicated time and space for meaningful conversations. This may involve setting aside regular date nights or engaging in activities that promote open and honest communication. It's also important to practice active listening and empathy, allowing our loved ones to feel heard and understood.

In addition to communication, emotional intimacy can be fostered through shared experiences and activities. Engaging in activities that bring joy and fulfillment to both partners can create a sense of connection and shared purpose. This may involve pursuing common interests, exploring new hobbies together, or simply spending quality time in each other's company.

The Role of Physical Intimacy

Physical intimacy is an important aspect of many intimate relationships. It involves a sense of closeness, affection, and sexual connection. Physical intimacy can enhance emotional intimacy and deepen the bond between partners.

To enhance physical intimacy, it's important to prioritize and prioritize the needs and desires of both partners. This involves open and honest communication about boundaries, desires, and preferences. It's also important to create a safe and comfortable environment where both partners feel free to express their desires and explore their sexuality.

Physical intimacy is not solely about sexual activity. It can also involve non-sexual forms of touch, such as cuddling, holding hands, or giving massages. These forms of physical affection can foster a sense of closeness and connection, even outside of the bedroom.

Overcoming Challenges

Enhancing intimacy and connection in relationships is not always easy. It requires effort, patience, and a willingness to confront and overcome challenges. Some common challenges that may arise include:

- Communication barriers: Misunderstandings, lack of effective communication skills, and differences in communication styles can hinder intimacy and connection. It's important to address these barriers by actively working on improving communication and seeking professional help if needed.
- Past wounds and traumas: Past experiences of hurt, betrayal, or trauma

can impact our ability to trust and connect with others. It's important to address and heal these wounds through therapy, self-reflection, and forgiveness.

- External stressors: External factors such as work stress, financial difficulties, or family issues can strain relationships and hinder intimacy. It's important to prioritize self-care and find healthy ways to manage stress in order to maintain a strong connection with our loved ones.

By acknowledging and addressing these challenges, we can create a solid foundation for enhancing intimacy and connection in our relationships. With patience, understanding, and a commitment to personal growth, we can cultivate deep and meaningful connections that bring joy, fulfillment, and solace to our lives.

7

Chapter 7

Navigating Different Types of Relationships

7.1 Romantic Relationships

Romantic relationships have the potential to bring immense joy, fulfillment, and growth into our lives. However, they can also be a source of confusion, conflict, and heartache. It is not uncommon for individuals to find themselves in a cycle of repeating patterns and unhealthy dynamics in their romantic relationships. In this section, we will explore the complexities of romantic relationships and provide insights and strategies for building healthy and lasting connections.

Understanding the Dynamics

Romantic relationships are unique in their intensity and emotional invest-ment. They often involve a deep level of vulnerability, trust, and intimacy. However, this level of closeness can also make romantic relationships more challenging to navigate. It is essential to understand the dynamics at play in order to build a strong foundation for a healthy and fulfilling romantic partnership.

One common challenge in romantic relationships is the tendency to repeat patterns from past relationships or childhood experiences. These patterns can manifest as a fear of intimacy, a need for control, or a tendency to attract partners who are emotionally unavailable. Recognizing these patterns is the first step towards breaking free from them and creating healthier dynamics.

Building Emotional Safety

Emotional safety is crucial in romantic relationships. It involves creating an environment where both partners feel secure, respected, and valued. Without emotional safety, it becomes difficult to express vulnerability, communicate effectively, and build trust. To foster emotional safety, it is important to cultivate open and honest communication, active listening, and empathy.

Creating emotional safety also requires setting and respecting boundaries. Boundaries help establish a sense of individuality and autonomy within the relationship. They allow each partner to express their needs, desires, and limits while respecting those of their partner. By maintaining healthy boundaries, both individuals can feel secure and supported in the relationship.

Developing Trust and Intimacy

Trust is the foundation of any healthy romantic relationship. It is built over time through consistent actions, open communication, and mutual respect. Trust allows individuals to feel safe and secure in sharing their thoughts, feelings, and vulnerabilities with their partner. Developing trust requires honesty, reliability, and a willingness to be vulnerable.

Intimacy goes hand in hand with trust. It involves emotional closeness, deep connection, and a sense of mutual understanding. Intimacy can be nurtured through open and authentic communication, spending quality time together, and engaging in activities that foster emotional connection. It is important to remember that intimacy is not solely limited to physical intimacy but encompasses emotional, intellectual, and spiritual connection as well.

Effective Communication

Communication is the lifeblood of any successful relationship, and romantic relationships are no exception. Effective communication involves both expressing oneself honestly and listening actively to one's partner. It requires being present, attentive, and empathetic. By practicing active listening, individuals can better understand their partner's needs, desires, and concerns, fostering a deeper sense of connection and understanding.

Expressing needs and desires is an essential aspect of communication in romantic relationships. It involves clearly and assertively communicating one's wants and needs while respecting the boundaries and needs of the partner. By expressing oneself authentically, individuals can avoid resentment and misunderstandings, creating a healthier and more fulfilling relationship.

Nurturing Romance and Connection

Romantic relationships thrive on romance and connection. It is important to prioritize and nurture these aspects to keep the relationship vibrant and fulfilling. This can be achieved through small gestures of love and appreciation, quality time spent together, and engaging in activities that bring joy and excitement to both partners.

Maintaining a sense of novelty and adventure in the relationship can also help keep the spark alive. Trying new experiences together, exploring shared interests, and supporting each other's personal growth and aspirations can contribute to a deepening sense of connection and fulfillment.

Resolving Conflict Constructively

Conflict is a natural part of any relationship, including romantic ones. However, how conflicts are handled can make a significant difference in the health and longevity of the relationship. It is important to approach conflicts with empathy, respect, and a willingness to find mutually beneficial solutions.

Constructive conflict resolution involves active listening, expressing oneself assertively yet respectfully, and seeking to understand the underlying needs and emotions of both partners. It also requires a commitment to finding common ground and working towards a resolution that honors the needs and values of both individuals.

In conclusion, romantic relationships have the potential to bring immense joy and fulfillment into our lives. By understanding the dynamics at play, building emotional safety, developing trust and intimacy, practicing effective communication, nurturing romance and connection, and resolving conflicts constructively, we can create and sustain healthy and lasting romantic relationships. Remember, it takes effort, commitment, and a willingness to grow together to build a relationship that stands the test of time.

7.2 Family Relationships

Family relationships are some of the most significant and influential connections we have in our lives. They shape our identity, provide a sense of belonging, and can greatly impact our emotional well-being. However, just like any other type of relationship, family dynamics can be complex and challenging to navigate. It is not uncommon for family relationships to be a source of both joy and conflict.

The Complexity of Family Relationships

Family relationships are unique because they are often characterized by a deep history and shared experiences. These connections can be incredibly rewarding, providing a support system and a sense of unconditional love. However, they can also be a source of tension and frustration. Family members may have different personalities, values, and expectations, which can lead to misunderstandings and conflicts.

Understanding Family Dynamics

To navigate family relationships effectively, it is essential to understand the dynamics at play. Each family has its own unique set of dynamics, influenced by factors such as cultural background, upbringing, and individual personalities. Some common dynamics include:

1. **Roles and Hierarchies:** Families often have established roles and hierarchies, with certain members taking on specific responsibilities or assuming leadership positions. These roles can influence how family members interact with one another and can sometimes lead to power imbalances or feelings of resentment.
2. **Communication Patterns:** Communication styles within families can vary significantly. Some families may have open and direct communication, while others may rely on more indirect or passive-aggressive communication. Understanding these patterns can help improve communication and reduce misunderstandings.
3. **Unresolved Issues:** Family relationships can be affected by unresolved issues from the past. These could include unresolved conflicts, past traumas, or unaddressed emotions. These unresolved issues can create tension and hinder the development of healthy relationships.

Building Healthy Family Relationships

While family relationships can be challenging, there are steps you can take to build healthier and more fulfilling connections with your family members. Here are some strategies to consider:

1. **Open and Honest Communication:** Effective communication is crucial in any relationship, including family relationships. Practice active listening, express your thoughts and feelings honestly, and encourage open dialogue. Avoid making assumptions and be willing to listen to different perspectives.

2. **Setting Boundaries:** Establishing clear boundaries is essential for maintaining healthy family relationships. Boundaries help define what is acceptable and what is not, and they promote respect and mutual understanding. Communicate your boundaries assertively and be willing to respect the boundaries of others.

3. **Resolving Conflict Constructively:** Conflict is inevitable in any relationship, but it is how we handle it that determines the outcome. Instead of avoiding or escalating conflicts, strive to resolve them constructively. Focus on finding common ground, practicing empathy, and seeking compromise.

4. **Practicing Forgiveness:** Forgiveness is a powerful tool for healing and strengthening family relationships. Holding onto grudges and resentments only perpetuates negativity and hinders growth. Practice forgiveness, both for yourself and for others, and strive to let go of past hurts.

5. **Seeking Support:** Sometimes, family relationships can become overwhelming, and seeking support from a therapist or counselor can be beneficial. A professional can provide guidance, help you navigate challenging dynamics, and offer tools for improving communication and resolving conflicts.

6. **Fostering Quality Time:** Make an effort to spend quality time with your family members. Engage in activities that promote bonding and create positive memories. This can include shared hobbies, family outings, or simply having meaningful conversations.

7. **Respecting Individual Differences:** Recognize and respect that each family member is an individual with their own unique perspectives, beliefs, and values. Embrace diversity within your family and foster an environment that encourages acceptance and understanding.

Embracing Change and Growth

Family relationships, like all relationships, are not static. They evolve and change over time. Embracing change and growth is essential for maintaining healthy family connections. As individuals grow and develop, their needs and expectations may shift. It is important to adapt to these changes and be open to new dynamics within the family.

Remember that building healthy family relationships takes time, effort, and patience. It requires a willingness to communicate, understand, and support one another. By prioritizing open communication, setting boundaries, resolving conflicts constructively, and fostering a sense of acceptance, you can cultivate stronger and more fulfilling family relationships.

7.3 Friendships

Friendships are an essential part of our lives. They provide us with companionship, support, and a sense of belonging. Unlike romantic relationships or family ties, friendships are often chosen connections that we make based on shared interests, values, and experiences. While friendships can bring immense joy and fulfillment, they can also be a source of conflict and frustration. In this section, we will explore the dynamics of friendships and discuss strategies for building and maintaining healthy and meaningful connections.

Understanding the Nature of Friendships

Friendships come in various forms and serve different purposes in our lives. Some friendships are casual and light-hearted, while others are deep and intimate. It is important to recognize that not all friendships will be the same, and that is perfectly okay. Each friendship has its own unique dynamics and expectations.

Friendships can be categorized into different types based on the level of closeness and intimacy. Acquaintances are people we know casually, such as colleagues or neighbors. While we may have friendly interactions with acquaintances, the level of emotional investment is typically low. Close friends, on the other hand, are those with whom we share a deeper bond. These are the friends we confide in, rely on for support, and spend quality time with. Close friendships often require more effort and investment, but they can also provide us with a greater sense of connection and understanding.

Nurturing Friendships

Like any relationship, friendships require effort and nurturing to thrive. Here are some strategies for building and maintaining healthy friendships:

1. Communication and Active Listening

Effective communication is the foundation of any successful friendship. It is important to be open, honest, and transparent with your friends. Express your thoughts, feelings, and needs clearly, and encourage your friends to do the same. Active listening is equally important. Give your full attention when your friends are speaking, and show empathy and understanding. Avoid interrupting or dismissing their feelings, as this can create barriers in the relationship.

2. Mutual Respect and Support

Respect is crucial in any friendship. Treat your friends with kindness, consideration, and respect their boundaries. Support them in their endeavors and celebrate their successes. Be there for them during challenging times and offer a listening ear or a helping hand. Remember that friendship is a two-way street, and both parties should contribute to the relationship.

3. Shared Interests and Activities

Shared interests and activities can strengthen the bond between friends. Engage in activities that you both enjoy, such as hobbies, sports, or volunteering. This not only provides opportunities for quality time together but also creates shared experiences and memories. It can also help to explore new interests together, as this can deepen the connection and provide opportunities for personal growth.

4. Trust and Loyalty

Trust is the cornerstone of any healthy friendship. Be reliable and trustworthy, keeping your promises and maintaining confidentiality. Trust takes time to build, so be patient and consistent in your actions. Similarly, loyalty is essential in friendships. Stand by your friends, support them in their decisions, and defend their honor when necessary. Trust and loyalty go hand in hand and are vital for the longevity of any friendship.

5. Resolving Conflict

Conflict is a natural part of any relationship, including friendships. It is important to address conflicts promptly and constructively. Avoiding or suppressing conflicts can lead to resentment and distance in the friendship. When conflicts arise, approach them with an open mind and a willingness to understand the other person's perspective. Communicate your feelings calmly and respectfully, and be open to finding a compromise or solution that works for both parties.

6. Boundaries and Independence

Respecting each other's boundaries is crucial in maintaining a healthy friendship. Understand and honor your friend's need for personal space, privacy, and autonomy. Avoid becoming overly dependent on your friend for emotional support or validation. It is important to maintain a sense of independence and have a diverse support system beyond just one friendship.

7. Quality Time and Regular Check-Ins

Investing quality time in your friendships is essential for their growth and maintenance. Make an effort to spend time together, whether it's through regular meetups, phone calls, or virtual hangouts. Prioritize your friendships and show your friends that they are important to you. Regular check-ins can also help you stay connected and aware of each other's lives, ensuring that the friendship remains strong.

Recognizing Toxic Friendships

While friendships can bring immense joy and support, it is important to be aware of toxic dynamics that can be detrimental to your well-being. Signs of a toxic friendship may include:

- Constant criticism or belittling
- Manipulative behavior
- Lack of respect for boundaries
- Frequent conflicts without resolution
- Feeling drained or emotionally exhausted after spending time with the friend
- Feeling like you have to constantly prove yourself or seek their approval

If you find yourself in a toxic friendship, it may be necessary to reassess the relationship and consider setting boundaries or, in some cases, ending the friendship for your own well-being.

Conclusion

Friendships are an integral part of our lives, providing us with companionship, support, and a sense of belonging. By understanding the nature of friendships and nurturing them with effective communication, mutual respect, shared interests, trust, and loyalty, we can build and sustain healthy and meaningful connections. Remember that friendships require effort and investment, but the rewards of having supportive and fulfilling relationships are well worth it.

7.4 Workplace Relationships

Workplace relationships play a significant role in our lives, as we spend a significant amount of time with our colleagues and superiors. These relationships can greatly impact our overall well-being and job satisfaction. Just like any other type of relationship, workplace relationships require effort, understanding, and effective communication to thrive. In this section, we will explore the dynamics of workplace relationships and provide strategies for building and maintaining healthy connections in the professional setting.

Understanding the Dynamics of Workplace Relationships

Workplace relationships can be complex due to the diverse personalities, backgrounds, and goals of individuals within an organization. It is essential to recognize that each person brings their own set of experiences, values, and communication styles to the workplace. Understanding these dynamics can help foster a more inclusive and supportive work environment.

One important aspect of workplace relationships is the power dynamics that exist within the organizational structure. Hierarchies, authority, and different levels of responsibility can influence how individuals interact with one another. It is crucial to be aware of these dynamics and strive for open and respectful communication, regardless of one's position within the organization.

Building Positive Workplace Relationships

Building positive workplace relationships is essential for creating a harmonious and productive work environment. Here are some strategies to foster healthy connections with your colleagues:

1. **Developing Empathy**: Empathy is the ability to understand and share the feelings of others. By putting yourself in your colleagues' shoes, you can gain a better understanding of their perspectives and challenges. This understanding can help you build stronger relationships based on compassion and support.

2. **Active Listening**: Actively listening to your colleagues demonstrates respect and shows that you value their opinions. Practice active listening by maintaining eye contact, nodding to show understanding, and asking clarifying questions. This approach fosters effective communication and helps build trust within the workplace.

3. **Collaboration and Teamwork**: Encouraging collaboration and teamwork can strengthen workplace relationships. By working together towards common goals, colleagues can develop a sense of camaraderie

and mutual respect. Foster a collaborative environment by promoting open communication, sharing credit for achievements, and recognizing the contributions of others.

4. **Resolving Conflicts Constructively**: Conflicts are inevitable in any workplace. However, it is essential to address conflicts in a constructive and respectful manner. Instead of avoiding or escalating conflicts, strive to find common ground and seek solutions that benefit all parties involved. Effective conflict resolution can lead to stronger relationships and a more harmonious work environment.

Navigating Different Roles and Hierarchies

Workplace relationships often involve navigating different roles and hierarchies. It is crucial to understand the expectations and boundaries associated with each role to maintain professionalism and respect. Here are some tips for navigating workplace relationships within different roles:

1. **Colleague to Colleague**: When interacting with colleagues at the same level, treat them as equals and show respect for their expertise and contributions. Foster a supportive and collaborative environment by offering assistance, sharing knowledge, and celebrating each other's successes.

2. **Supervisor to Subordinate**: As a supervisor, it is important to provide clear expectations, constructive feedback, and support to your subordinates. Encourage open communication, listen to their concerns, and provide opportunities for growth and development. Building a positive and trusting relationship with your subordinates can enhance productivity and job satisfaction.

3. **Subordinate to Supervisor**: When interacting with your supervisor, maintain professionalism and respect their authority. Communicate openly about your work progress, challenges, and goals. Seek feedback and guidance to improve your performance and demonstrate your commitment to the organization's success.

4. **Cross-Departmental Relationships**: In a larger organization, you may need to collaborate with colleagues from different departments. Building relationships across departments can enhance communication, problem-solving, and overall efficiency. Take the initiative to reach out, understand their roles and responsibilities, and find common ground to foster effective collaboration.

Dealing with Workplace Challenges

Workplace relationships can face various challenges that can impact productivity and job satisfaction. Here are some common challenges and strategies for addressing them:

1. **Conflict and Miscommunication**: Misunderstandings and conflicts can arise due to differences in communication styles, expectations, or work approaches. To address these challenges, practice active listening, clarify expectations, and communicate openly and respectfully. If conflicts persist, consider involving a mediator or seeking guidance from a supervisor or HR department.
2. **Workplace Politics**: Office politics can create tension and strain workplace relationships. To navigate workplace politics, focus on maintaining professionalism, staying neutral, and avoiding gossip or negative conversations. Instead, prioritize building positive relationships based on trust.

8

Chapter 8

Sustaining Healthy Relationships

8.1 Practicing Self-Care in Relationships

In the midst of navigating the complexities of relationships, it is crucial to prioritize self-care. Our closest relationships can sometimes become a source of crisis rather than solace. Whether it is a romantic partner, a parent, child, friend, or colleague, the dynamics can often feel stagnant, leaving us yearning for change. However, it is important to recognize that change begins within ourselves. By practicing self-care in relationships, we can create a foundation of love, understanding, and growth.

The Importance of Self-Care

Self-care is not selfish; it is a necessary component of maintaining healthy relationships. When we neglect our own well-being, we may find ourselves feeling drained, resentful, and unable to fully show up for others. By prioritizing self-care, we are better equipped to meet the needs of our loved ones while also nurturing our own emotional, mental, and physical health.

Setting Boundaries

One essential aspect of self-care in relationships is setting and maintaining boundaries. Boundaries are the guidelines we establish to protect our emotional and physical well-being. They help us define what is acceptable and what is not in our relationships. By clearly communicating our boundaries, we create a safe space for ourselves and others to navigate the dynamics of the relationship.

Setting boundaries involves recognizing our limits and communicating them assertively. It is important to remember that boundaries are not meant to control or manipulate others but rather to ensure that our needs are respected. By setting boundaries, we establish a sense of self-worth and create an environment where healthy communication and mutual respect can thrive.

Prioritizing Emotional Well-being

Emotional well-being is a vital aspect of self-care in relationships. It involves acknowledging and honoring our emotions while also recognizing the emotions of others. It is essential to create a safe space for open and honest communication, allowing both parties to express their feelings without judgment or criticism.

Practicing emotional self-care involves self-reflection and self-awareness. It requires us to identify and process our own emotions, understanding their origins and impact on our relationships. By taking responsibility for our emotional well-being, we can approach our relationships with empathy, compassion, and understanding.

Practicing Active Listening

Active listening is a powerful tool for self-care in relationships. It involves fully engaging with the speaker, giving them our undivided attention, and seeking to understand their perspective without interrupting or judging. By practicing active listening, we demonstrate respect and validation for the other person's thoughts and feelings.

To practice active listening, we can focus on the speaker's words, body language, and tone of voice. We can also ask clarifying questions to ensure that we have understood their message accurately. By actively listening, we foster a deeper connection and create an environment where both parties feel heard and valued.

Taking Time for Self-Reflection

Self-reflection is an essential practice for self-care in relationships. It involves taking the time to examine our thoughts, feelings, and behaviors within the context of our relationships. By engaging in self-reflection, we gain insight into our patterns, triggers, and areas for personal growth.

During moments of self-reflection, we can ask ourselves questions such as:

- How do I contribute to the dynamics of this relationship?
- Are there any unresolved emotions or past wounds that are affecting my interactions?
- Am I effectively communicating my needs and desires?
- Are there any unhealthy habits or patterns that I need to address?

By honestly examining ourselves, we can identify areas where we can improve and take proactive steps towards personal growth and development.

Practicing Self-Compassion

Self-compassion is a fundamental aspect of self-care in relationships. It involves treating ourselves with kindness, understanding, and acceptance, especially during challenging times. By practicing self-compassion, we cultivate a sense of inner peace and resilience, which positively impacts our relationships.

To practice self-compassion, we can:

- Practice self-care activities that bring us joy and relaxation.
- Challenge negative self-talk and replace it with positive affirmations.
- Forgive ourselves for past mistakes and embrace our imperfections.
- Set realistic expectations and avoid self-judgment.
- Surround ourselves with a supportive network of friends and loved ones.

By nurturing ourselves with self-compassion, we create a solid foundation from which we can build and sustain healthy relationships.

Balancing Independence and Interdependence

Maintaining a healthy balance between independence and interdependence is crucial for self-care in relationships. While it is important to nurture our individuality and pursue our own passions and interests, it is equally important to foster connection and collaboration within our relationships.

Balancing independence involves honoring our own needs, desires, and boundaries. It means taking responsibility for our own happiness and not relying solely on others for fulfillment. On the other hand, interdependence involves recognizing the value of collaboration, compromise, and shared experiences within our relationships.

By finding this balance, we create a harmonious dynamic where both parties can grow individually while also supporting and uplifting each other.

Conclusion

Practicing self-care in relationships is essential for building and sustaining healthy connections. By setting boundaries, prioritizing emotional well-being, practicing active listening, engaging in self-reflection, and cultivating self-compassion, we create a solid foundation for growth and understanding. Balancing independence and interdependence allows us to nurture our individuality while fostering connection within our relationships. By prioritizing self-care, we can transform our relationships into sources of love, support, and fulfillment.

8.2 Maintaining Balance and Independence

Maintaining balance and independence is crucial in sustaining healthy relationships. While it is natural to invest time and energy into our relationships, it is equally important to prioritize our own well-being and individuality. When we neglect our own needs and become overly dependent on others, it can lead to feelings of resentment, frustration, and a loss of personal identity. In this section, we will explore the significance of maintaining balance and independence in relationships and discuss practical strategies to achieve this.

The Importance of Balance

Finding balance in relationships involves striking a harmonious equilibrium between our own needs and the needs of our partners or loved ones. It is essential to recognize that we are individuals with unique desires, goals, and interests. Neglecting our own needs in favor of constantly catering to others can lead to feelings of burnout and dissatisfaction. By maintaining a healthy balance, we can ensure that our relationships are mutually fulfilling and sustainable.

Embracing Independence

Independence within relationships does not imply detachment or disengagement. Instead, it refers to maintaining a sense of self and individuality while being part of a partnership or connection. It is crucial to nurture our own passions, hobbies, and personal growth alongside our relationships. When we have a strong sense of self, we bring more to the table in our interactions with others, fostering a healthier and more fulfilling dynamic.

Setting Boundaries

One of the key aspects of maintaining balance and independence is setting and enforcing boundaries. Boundaries define what is acceptable and what is not in our relationships. They help us establish limits and communicate our needs effectively. By setting boundaries, we create a framework that allows us to prioritize our well-being and maintain a healthy level of independence. It is important to communicate these boundaries clearly and assertively, ensuring that they are respected by both ourselves and our loved ones.

Prioritizing Self-Care

Self-care is an essential component of maintaining balance and independence in relationships. It involves taking deliberate actions to nurture our physical, emotional, and mental well-being. Engaging in activities that bring us joy, practicing mindfulness, and prioritizing rest and relaxation are all crucial aspects of self-care. By prioritizing self-care, we replenish our energy and maintain a healthy sense of self, enabling us to show up fully in our relationships.

Cultivating Supportive Networks

Maintaining balance and independence also involves cultivating supportive networks outside of our primary relationships. Having a diverse social circle allows us to engage in different activities, explore new interests, and seek support from multiple sources. It is important to nurture friendships, engage in community activities, and build connections with like-minded individuals. These external relationships provide us with additional perspectives, support, and a sense of belonging, enhancing our overall well-being and independence.

Honoring Personal Goals and Aspirations

Maintaining balance and independence requires us to honor our personal goals and aspirations. It is essential to have a clear understanding of our own values, dreams, and ambitions. By pursuing our individual goals alongside our relationships, we create a sense of fulfillment and purpose. This not only benefits us personally but also enriches our relationships as we bring our passions and achievements into the shared space.

Effective Time Management

Balancing our personal lives and relationships requires effective time management. It is important to allocate time for ourselves, our relationships, and other commitments in a way that feels balanced and sustainable. This may involve setting aside dedicated "me time," scheduling quality time with loved ones, and prioritizing tasks and responsibilities. By managing our time effectively, we can ensure that we have the necessary space and energy to maintain our independence while nurturing our relationships.

Open and Honest Communication

Maintaining balance and independence in relationships relies on open and honest communication. It is crucial to express our needs, desires, and concerns to our partners or loved ones. By fostering a safe and non-judgmental environment for communication, we can ensure that our individuality is respected and valued. Effective communication allows us to negotiate boundaries, discuss personal goals, and find mutually beneficial solutions that support both our independence and the health of our relationships.

Flexibility and Adaptability

Lastly, maintaining balance and independence requires flexibility and adaptability. Relationships are dynamic, and circumstances change over time. It is important to be open to adjusting our expectations, boundaries, and priorities as needed. Flexibility allows us to navigate the evolving nature of relationships while maintaining our sense of self and independence. By embracing change and being willing to adapt, we can sustain healthy and fulfilling connections with our loved ones.

In conclusion, maintaining balance and independence is vital for sustaining healthy relationships. By prioritizing our own well-being, setting boundaries, practicing self-care, and nurturing our individuality, we can create a harmonious equilibrium between our personal needs and the needs of our relationships. Effective time management, open communication, and flexibility also play crucial roles in maintaining this balance. By embracing these strategies, we can cultivate relationships that are mutually fulfilling, supportive, and sustainable.

8.3 Continuing Personal Growth and Development

In order to sustain healthy relationships, it is essential to prioritize personal growth and development. While it is common to focus on the growth and development of the relationship itself, neglecting personal growth can hinder the progress and fulfillment within the relationship. By continuing to grow and develop as individuals, we can bring new perspectives, skills, and insights into our relationships, fostering a sense of growth and vitality.

Embracing Self-Reflection

One of the key aspects of personal growth and development is self-reflection. Taking the time to reflect on our thoughts, emotions, and behaviors allows us to gain a deeper understanding of ourselves and our patterns in relationships. Self-reflection helps us identify areas where we may need to grow and change, as well as recognize our strengths and values.

Engaging in self-reflection can be done through various practices such as journaling, meditation, or seeking therapy. These practices provide a space for introspection and self-awareness, enabling us to identify any limiting beliefs or negative patterns that may be affecting our relationships. By becoming more aware of ourselves, we can make conscious choices to improve and evolve.

Pursuing Personal Interests and Passions

Continuing personal growth and development involves pursuing our own interests and passions outside of our relationships. It is important to maintain a sense of individuality and autonomy, as this contributes to our overall well-being and happiness. When we engage in activities that bring us joy and fulfillment, we bring a sense of vitality and enthusiasm into our relationships.

By pursuing personal interests, we also expand our knowledge and experiences, which can enhance our conversations and connections with others. Sharing our passions with our loved ones can deepen our bond and create opportunities for growth and learning together. Additionally, having our own interests and passions can provide a sense of fulfillment and purpose, which ultimately contributes to our overall satisfaction in life and relationships.

Seeking Personal Development Opportunities

Personal growth and development can be further nurtured by actively seeking opportunities for learning and self-improvement. This can involve attending workshops, seminars, or classes that align with our interests and goals. Engaging in personal development activities allows us to acquire new skills, broaden our perspectives, and challenge ourselves to grow.

Additionally, reading books, listening to podcasts, or engaging in online courses can provide valuable insights and knowledge that can be applied to our personal growth journey. By continuously seeking personal development opportunities, we demonstrate a commitment to our own growth and inspire those around us to do the same.

Cultivating Emotional Intelligence

Emotional intelligence plays a crucial role in sustaining healthy relationships. It involves the ability to recognize, understand, and manage our own emotions, as well as empathize with the emotions of others. By cultivating emotional intelligence, we can navigate conflicts, communicate effectively, and build deeper connections with our loved ones.

Developing emotional intelligence requires self-awareness and empathy. It involves being able to identify and regulate our own emotions, as well as being attuned to the emotions of others. Practicing active listening, expressing empathy, and validating the emotions of our loved ones can foster a sense of emotional safety and trust within the relationship.

Setting and Revisiting Personal Goals

Continuing personal growth and development involves setting and revisiting personal goals. These goals can be related to various aspects of our lives, such as career, health, relationships, or personal hobbies. By setting goals, we provide ourselves with a sense of direction and purpose, which can contribute to our overall growth and fulfillment.

It is important to regularly revisit and reassess our goals to ensure they align with our evolving values and aspirations. As we grow and change, our goals may need to be adjusted or expanded. By regularly evaluating our progress and making necessary adjustments, we can stay on track with our personal growth journey and continue to evolve as individuals.

Practicing Self-Compassion

Personal growth and development require patience and self-compassion. It is important to acknowledge that growth is a lifelong process and that setbacks and challenges are a natural part of the journey. Practicing self-compassion involves treating ourselves with kindness, understanding, and forgiveness.

When faced with obstacles or setbacks, it is important to approach ourselves with self-compassion rather than self-criticism. By embracing our imperfections and learning from our mistakes, we create a nurturing environment for personal growth. Self-compassion also allows us to extend compassion and understanding to others, fostering healthier and more fulfilling relationships.

In conclusion, continuing personal growth and development is essential for sustaining healthy relationships. By embracing self-reflection, pursuing personal interests, seeking personal development opportunities, cultivating emotional intelligence, setting and revisiting personal goals, and practicing self-compassion, we can foster personal growth and bring new energy and vitality into our relationships. Prioritizing personal growth not only benefits ourselves but also contributes to the overall health and longevity of our relationships.

8.4 Nurturing and Celebrating Relationships

Building and sustaining healthy relationships requires ongoing effort and dedication. It is not enough to simply establish boundaries, communicate effectively, and cultivate self-love. Nurturing and celebrating relationships is an essential aspect of maintaining long-lasting connections with others. In this section, we will explore various strategies and practices that can help you nurture and celebrate your relationships.

8.4.1 Cultivating Appreciation and Gratitude

One of the most effective ways to nurture and celebrate your relationships is by cultivating appreciation and gratitude. Take the time to acknowledge and express gratitude for the people in your life who bring you joy, support, and love. This can be done through simple acts of kindness, such as sending a heartfelt thank-you note or expressing your appreciation verbally. By showing gratitude, you not only strengthen your bond with others but also enhance your own sense of happiness and fulfillment.

8.4.2 Quality Time and Active Presence

In our fast-paced and busy lives, it is easy to get caught up in the demands of work, responsibilities, and distractions. However, nurturing relationships requires intentional effort and quality time spent together. Make it a priority to carve out dedicated time for your loved ones, free from distractions and interruptions. Engage in activities that promote connection and create meaningful memories. Whether it's going for a walk, having a meal together, or engaging in a shared hobby, the key is to be fully present and attentive during these moments.

8.4.3 Effective Communication and Active Listening

Effective communication is crucial for nurturing relationships. It involves not only expressing your thoughts and feelings but also actively listening to others. Practice active listening by giving your full attention, maintaining eye contact, and showing empathy and understanding. Avoid interrupting or jumping to conclusions. By fostering open and honest communication, you create a safe space for both parties to express themselves and deepen their connection.

8.4.4 Acts of Kindness and Thoughtfulness

Small acts of kindness and thoughtfulness can go a long way in nurturing relationships. Surprise your loved ones with gestures that show you care, such as preparing their favorite meal, leaving them a heartfelt note, or offering a helping hand when they need it. These acts of kindness not only demonstrate your love and support but also strengthen the bond between you and your loved ones.

8.4.5 Celebrating Milestones and Achievements

Celebrating milestones and achievements is an important part of nurturing relationships. Take the time to acknowledge and celebrate the successes and accomplishments of your loved ones. Whether it's a promotion at work, a personal achievement, or a special occasion, make an effort to show your support and share in their joy. This can be done through simple gestures like sending a congratulatory message, organizing a small gathering, or giving a thoughtful gift. By celebrating together, you reinforce the importance of their happiness and create lasting memories.

8.4.6 Honoring Individuality and Autonomy

While nurturing relationships involves spending quality time together and engaging in shared activities, it is equally important to honor individuality and autonomy. Recognize and respect the unique interests, goals, and boundaries of your loved ones. Encourage them to pursue their passions and dreams, even if they differ from your own. By supporting their individuality, you create a space for personal growth and self-expression within the relationship.

8.4.7 Resolving Conflict with Compassion

Conflict is a natural part of any relationship, but how it is handled can greatly impact its health and longevity. When conflicts arise, approach them with compassion and a willingness to understand the other person's perspective. Practice active listening, empathy, and open-mindedness. Seek resolution through constructive dialogue and compromise, rather than resorting to blame or defensiveness. By resolving conflicts with compassion, you strengthen the foundation of trust and understanding within the relationship.

8.4.8 Expressing Love and Affection

Expressing love and affection is a fundamental aspect of nurturing relationships. Find ways to show your love and affection to your loved ones regularly. This can be done through verbal expressions of love, physical touch, acts of service, or giving thoughtful gifts. The key is to consistently demonstrate your love and appreciation for the people in your life. By doing so, you create a nurturing and loving environment that fosters deep connections and emotional intimacy.

8.4.9 Practicing Empathic Understanding and Letting Go

This is an essential component of nurturing relationships. Holding onto grudges and resentments can poison the connection between you and your loved ones. Practice empathic understanding by letting go of past hurts and embracing a mindset of compassion and understanding. This does not mean condoning harmful behavior but rather choosing to release the negative emotions associated with it. By practicing this, you create space for healing and growth within the relationship.

8.4.10 Prioritizing Self-Care and Well-being

Lastly, nurturing relationships requires prioritizing self-care and well-being. Take care of yourself physically, mentally, and emotionally, as this directly impacts your ability to show up fully in your relationships. Set boundaries, practice self-compassion, and engage in activities that bring you joy and fulfillment. By prioritizing your own well-being, you not only enhance your own happiness but also create a positive ripple effect on your relationships.

In conclusion, nurturing and celebrating relationships is an ongoing process that requires intentional effort and dedication. By cultivating appreciation and gratitude, spending quality time together, practicing effective communication, and expressing love and affection, you can strengthen the bonds with your loved ones. Additionally, honoring individuality, resolving conflicts with compassion, and practicing empathic understanding contributes to the health and longevity of relationships. Remember to prioritize self-care and well-being, as this forms the foundation for nurturing and sustaining healthy connections.

II

Final Word

Embarking on a journey of developing your authentic self is not without it's difficulties. People close to you might start to push back as you begin to set boundaries and express your needs. Those who want you to be happy will embrace this change. Never be afraid to reach out for professional help with a therapist or psychologist who can help you navigate this journey.

About the Author

Sara grew up in a small coastal town in the Hunter Valley region in NSW, Australia. She experienced sexism, homophobia, and the pressure to conform to heteronormative standards of the time; at home, at school and by the parochial attitudes of the local coastal community. She moved to the big city to find freedom, develop her long held passions, create change and develop her authentic self. She has studied clinical and forensic psychology, taught at university and worked in community corrections.

Also by Sara L. Weston

The following book can be used as a companion book to 'Authenticity Unveiled'.

Authentic Love: A Guide to Creating Healthy Lesbian Relationships.
Eight chapter road-map to finding your authentic self and partner.